Alain-Fournier: A Brief Life

Also by David Arkell
from Carcanet

Looking for Laforgue

ALAIN-FOURNIER
A Brief Life
(1886-1914)

David Arkell

CARCANET

First published in Great Britain 1986 by
Carcanet Press Limited
208-212 Corn Exchange Buildings
Manchester M4 3BQ

and 108 East 31st Street
New York, New York 10016

The publishers acknowledge the assistance
of the Arts Council of Great Britain

British Library Cataloguing in Publication Data
Arkell, David
    Alain-Fournier : a brief life.
    1. Alain-Fournier — Biography
    2. Novelists, French — 20th century — Biography
    I. Title
    843'.912   PQ2611.085Z/

    ISBN 0-85635-484-8

Typesetting by Koinonia Limited, Manchester
Printed in England by SRP Ltd, Exeter

Contents

Acknowledgements

My special thanks to Alain Rivière, the nephew of Alain-Fournier and son of Jacques Rivière. As Alain-Fournier's literary executor he read the text in manuscript and – while not responsible for my interpretations – has ensured that the basic facts are correct. He has also provided, from his unique collection, the best of my illustrations. Some are reproduced here for the first time, others have appeared in the *Bulletin des Amis de Jacques Rivière et d'Alain-Fournier*, a quarterly publication issued from 31 rue Arthur-Petit, 78220 – Viroflay, France. My thanks also to MM. Jean Loize and Yves Rey-Herme.

References to the source of quotations are given at the end of the book, and I am most grateful for the kind co-operation of the publishers involved: Editions Gallimard, Arthème Fayard, Hachette and Alphée.

1 · *Country boy (1886-1903)*

They used to say that the smart thing to do, if you were an ambitious child in France, was to choose an *instituteur* as father.

The humble *instituteur*, or primary-school teacher, stood for a 'certain idea' of France (though not de Gaulle's). He was the anti-clerical offspring of the French Revolution and in tune with its essential virtues. Men like the writer Charles Péguy saw the *instituteur* – in his heyday – as the keeper of the nation's conscience, whose devotion to the common interest was the supreme instrument of social indoctrination.

This selfless paragon of civic duty was also doing himself a favour. To become an *instituteur* was the established way for a bright child of poor parents to get on in the world. Why waste time at a *lycée* passing the *baccalauréat* when you could go straight to the local teacher-trainer college (*École Normale d'instituteurs*) and get on with a career?

Péguy, indeed, waxed lyrical on the subject of those student-teachers: in their sombre frock-coats he saw them as the dashing black hussars of the Republic – comparable to the famous *cadre noir* of the Saumur cavalry school. And after the trainee-*instituteur* had left the *École Normale* it was normal, too, for him to marry the *institutrice*, and share the accommodation that the State provided. It made sense.

Alain-Fournier's parents were typical *instituteurs*. As such they were pillars of the community in their different ways. Part of the schoolhouse was given over to the archives, where villagers intending to wed had to go and register their names (since the schoolmaster was officially an adjunct of the mayor). But since he was also, almost by definition, a rationalist, he could not be seen to be over-concerned with religion. Here was where his wife stepped in. If Madame chose to mingle with the locals in occasional aspects of church life, that was her affair – at these moments Monsieur went fishing.

As befits a teacher's son, Henri Fournier was born obligingly at the beginning of the school year, on 3 October 1886. He also had the prescience – as one of the most French of French writers – to arrive in the still centre of France itself: the Cher department. French departments are often named after the rivers that run through them. The valley of the Cher is the heartland of old Berry province.

Henri at eighteen months, spring 1888

Fournier's childhood was as calm and peaceful as that old Berry province itself, which used to figure in illuminated manuscripts representing the serene landscape of France during the four seasons of the year. Similarly the *très riches heures* that Henri spent there embodied the typically French virtue of *mesure* (nothing in excess). The religion he picked up from his mother was something more like a mood or attitude than a faith. The education his father distilled was the basic French cultural background and from his immediate contemporaries he acquired Gallic *savoir-vivre*. All these qualities are evident in François Seurel, the narrator of *Le Grand Meaulnes*.[1]

'I am a peasant', said Henri Fournier. 'I must confess that sometimes I'm embarrassed by the faults that peasants have; and sometimes I'm embarrassed by my own peasant-faults.' But that is far from the whole story, for he was a country boy who stormed Paris, wrote a bestseller and won the love of a famous actress. He was an outgoing personality, a brilliant athlete, the scourge of school-teachers and the Establishment in general, yet all his life he remained an abnormally sensitive man. These were just some of the contradictions in his character.

He was indeed François Seurel, the narrator of *Le Grand Meaulnes*. But in a more dashing and adventurous persona he was also Augustin Meaulnes himself, And, finally, he was that somewhat immature other character Frantz de Galais, who might be termed the Author as a Spoilt Brat (which at times he undoubtedly was).

Three villages in the Cher were touched by the spell of Fournier: Epineuil-le-Fleuriel, La Chapelle d'Angillon and Nançay. La Chapelle, in the extreme north, was his mother's family home: here he was born, and here he spent the holidays later on. But when he was five, the family moved to a new school, far to the south, at Epineuil. At Epineuil Henri spent the formative years of his life, between the ages of five and twelve.

As for Nançay, it was the place where he spent Septembers and which epitomized for him the Sologne, that district of France he loved above all others. It is a flat land of heath and marshes, which had once been the home of Huguenots but in Fournier's day lay abandoned. Eighteenth-century persecution had left it with many empty dwellings, and even châteaux, which helped give it an air of mystery. Its other characteristic

[1] Alain-Fournier's *Le Grand Meaulnes* was first published in 1913, but all references here are to the Livre de Poche edition of 1983. The author's hyphenated pseudonym was a literary device used by him from 1907 onwards. The book's title, which originally gave some trouble to French critics, is pronounced more or less like the English word 'moan'.

EPINEUIL (Cher). - Un jour de Foire

1. EPINEUIL-LE-FLEURIEL (Cher). — Route de Maulne

was monotony: Rimbaud once referred to 'a hundred Solognes as long as a railway'.

It would be fruitless to describe Fournier's idyllic childhood at Epineuil, since he did not recognize it as such at the time; it was rather in memory that it seemed so. He wrote a curious letter from London when he was eighteen, in which he says: 'I no longer know if it is the countryside itself that I miss, or that time in the past which I spent there. The feeling I get, very gentle and very deep, could be called nostalgia for the past.' This solemn pronouncement seems almost to claim that he invented nostalgia – and perhaps in a way he did: few people, certainly, have ever felt it so keenly, or become so obsessed with it. The past – not necessarily as it was, but as it seems to have been – kept beckoning him back to his childhood. Indeed, those days in the Cher were not fully exorcised until he wrote the haunting novel describing them.

Fournier's sister Isabelle was three years younger than he, and the intensity of their life together at Épineuil helps to explain the closeness of their subsequent relationship. Their happiest times were spent reading the books to be given out as prizes, which arrived in crates addressed to their father towards the end of the school year. All those adventure stories, many of them English, teased their imaginations and, sharing so many secrets, they grew up as close as twins. When Isabelle later married his best friend, Henri was distressed to the point almost of nervous depression. Isabelle, for her part, often found it difficult to accept his women friends, and, in the case of the last one, her antagonism was intense. Her feelings on these occasions seemed more maternal than sisterly: the loving anxiety of a mother who thinks that no woman is worthy of her boy.

It appears from old photographs that Épineuil in those days was full of flowers, and it is certain that, when Henri returned there in imagination, there were more flowers still. Life was ruled by that excellent pike-fisherman M. Fournier and his charming hat-making wife. For the long summer holiday each year the family went off to La Chapelle, where Henri's beloved maternal grandmother 'Maman-Barthe' still lived. Come September they would move on to Nançay, where the hostess was M. Fournier's sister Augustine Raimbault.

Today the site of a famous radio-telescope, Nançay is only twelve miles from La Chapelle, but in those days it seemed much farther. Isabelle writes with surprise that there were roads on the western edge of La Chapelle where you could already feel the Sologne beginning. 'On the road to Presly, soon after you leave La Chapelle, there's a steep hill and then you reach the fir plantation, the birch woods, the stretches of purple heather and solitude.' Fournier called the Sologne 'useless, silent and profound'.

The Raimbaults had eight daughters, the eldest of whom – Marie-Rose – was a special favourite of Henri's. He was always miserable when for some reason, a family tiff maybe, he missed seeing her. Marie-Rose would eventually appear, like everyone and everything he ever loved, in *Le Grand Meaulnes*.

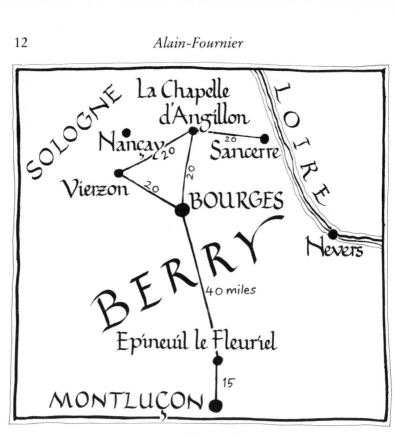

Epineuil: the schoolhouse

Class at Epineuil, c. 1900.
First row (centre): Isabelle Fournier

At the age of twelve Fournier was banished from paradise, being sent away to continue his education at one of the great Paris lycées, the Lycée Voltaire. His mother would scarcely have let him go if she had not known that an old neighbour from Epineuil, Mme Gabrielle Bijard, was living near the school at 196 rue de la Roquette. Fournier later remembered the sad Sunday mornings he spent there, in the courtyard (all now demolished) of No. 196, where the hurdy-gurdy men used to come and grind out their melancholy tunes. 'During those first three years I hated Paris with the hatred of a peasant,' he said, though a photograph taken of him aged thirteen in 1899 shows him adapting pretty well: with his almost shaved head he looks a tough little Parisian and not without a certain style. Mme Bijard ran a girls' school and he was at the same time sharpening his wits against some of the little Parisiennes, whom at first he found intimidating.

The atmosphere of the district surrounding the lycée and Mme Bijard's school left its mark on Fournier. Adjoining the cemetery of Père-Lachaise, with the Boulevard Ménilmontant running alongside, it is one of the hubs of working-class Paris and the scene of the great tragedy of the Commune: a tragedy which, in those days, was only thirty years old. The prison of La Grande Roquette was still standing, just down the road from No. 196. Fournier knew it well and saw it demolished. 'There was never an epoch more Shakespearean,' he said later. 'Imagine those things happening in the Place Voltaire!'

While claiming to hate Paris on that first visit, he was already preparing to love it. . . just as soon as he could look back on it with nostalgia. Consider these three separate confessions much later to his friend Jacques Rivière:

> I love the Parisian working-man, who's so different from the peasant in his independence and lack of respect: so pitilessly logical, yet altogether as serious as the peasant when it comes to his job or politics, which are indeed things to be pitilessly logical about [. . .] I always feel at home in a gathering of working-men. I can respond to them in the way they like, with the sympathetic phrase. . .

> It must be because I lived near the Boulevard Ménilmontant that I never lost the desire – as fervent, important and beautiful as any other – to know those people, for whom the most wonderful and exotic of landscapes is the Gingerbread Fair with its sordid sideshows and squalid crowds, whence you see emerging pasty-faced children perched high on shoulders. . . and where there suddenly passes some tragic countenance, horribly tumefied. In my book there'll be those people [. . .] but I'm well aware how far from Christian my book will be: an attempt to construct without faith a whole world of wonder and mystery. . .

> On the day of Mi-Carême [mid-Lent] I told my friends that I wasn't going to join the crowds; then as usual, in the evening, I found myself on the Place de l'Hôtel-de-Ville, stuck in the front row. I like ordinary people more than I can say when I'm lost in the middle of them like that, when there's nothing of my own life and milieu to separate me from them.

These remarks had their origin during the three years he spent in the East End of Paris, hating it all the time. It was about now that his mother gave him his first 9 x 12cm camera, which he learnt to use with skill. One longs to find examples of his early work in Paris, showing scenes in the eleventh Arrondissement at the turn of the century, but none has ever turned up. What we do have, however, is a splendid set of pictures taken in the country and reproduced here – many of them for the first time, including that evocative shot of the *grande place* at Epineuil (when it still had trees) seen from the schoolhouse attics in 1899. In the book about their childhood together, Isabelle has described their excitement as this picture slowly revealed itself in the developing tank 'with the esplanade of lime trees and the tower of the notary's house in the background'.[1] Here, too is the thirteen-year-old photographer himself in a sailor-suit and crew-cut.

Henri at the Lycée Voltaire, spring 1900

Isabelle, too, was sent to Paris at this time, in order to have treatment for a dislocated hip at the old Hôpital Trousseau. One of Fournier's letters dated 13 December 1898, reports a visit to her: 'I saw Isabelle today, and stayed with her for an hour. She's very well and told me all about her little affairs. She's going to have an operation at the end of the month. Meanwhile she's happy and sings all day,'

[1]Isabelle Rivière: *Images d'Alain-Fournier* (Emile-Paul, 1938), p. 161.

Henri in naval uniform, Brest, 1902

The French have a word – *correspondant* – for which there is no English equivalent: it means a friend who acts *in loco parentis* for a child who is, for instance, away at school. Henri's *correspondant* was Léopold Bernard, who lived in a comfortable flat at 25 avenue de la République. He became indispensable to the family for a very French reason: he had the ear of a certain M. Albert Thomas who in turn knew ministers and who could, like a fairy godfather who is also a conjuror, produce the most unlikely favours from his top hat. M. Bernard had two sons, of whom the younger, Jean, became one of Henri's best friends. Together they explored the Paris exhibition of 1900, and it was to Jean that Henri confided his wish to become a sailor. Nobody took much notice at the time, but Fournier had a way of making things happen: on the eve of his fifteenth birthday he applied for a transfer to a lycée at Brest, where he would prepare for the entrance exam to the training ship *Borda*.

Henri's letters home from Brest follow a pattern which was

to become familiar: he discovers, too late, that – compared to this Brittany outpost and his brutal companions – the rue de la Roquette had been a paradise. 'Brest is an old sad town, and the lycée a great monument like a barracks.' he wrote on 30 September 1901. And a little later: 'Have I told you that it rains here, on an average, every day?' Later still he put it in an alexandrine: 'For it has rained. . . it rains . . . it will rain every day.' This is the town, indeed, about which Jacques Prévert wrote, 'Rappelle-toi, Barbara, il pleuvait sans cesse sur Brest ce jour-là.'

One such rainy day was remembered by Fournier in his story 'La Femme empoisonnée'. It was a Thursday half-holiday, but the afternoon walk had been cancelled and the boys wandered disconsolately through the great sweating building. They were watching the rain from the dormitory windows when 'suddenly we turned and saw the headmaster's daughter dash out of the linen room, her skipping rope tied round her waist and the wooden ends chocking together as she ran.' Here was a girl to dream about 'with her black apron and her hair pulled back in a short pigtail.' It was also about now that Fournier chose to read Eugène Fromentin's *Dominique*, but more of that later.

On the day he took delivery of his navy-blue uniform with the twin gold anchors on the collar, he reported to his parents that it suited him. But there was little else that suited him at Brest. 'Every morning at 5.30 we jump from bed on the first roll of a drum.' The Bretons, he finds, are 'a wild people'. Too wild, it seems, for Fournier, who, after passing the first part of his *bachot* exam, made another of his sudden decisions: other people could become sailors and see the world. For himself, he would go back to the Cher, which is about as far as you can get from the sea without actually leaving France.

True to his nature, of course, he came to love the sea once he had left it. *Le Grand Meaulnes* is full of sea images: and Frantz de Galais, one of Fournier's *alter egos,* is a man with the sea in his blood.

So Fournier passed the second part of his baccalauréat exam at Bourges, a lycée which was later named after him. He was there for only two terms and had two girl-friends, whom he always remembered later as walking round the bandstand, 'one with a white sunshade, the other with blue eyes'.

Bourges is the principal town of the Cher, as well as the ancient capital of Berry province. When homesick he would intone the names of the railway stations linking Bourges with la Chapelle d'Angillon, twenty miles to the north. They formed a roll-call of nostalgia and a charm to conjure away anxiety: 'Asnières, Arrêt de Fussy, Saint-Martin-Saint-Georges, Menetou-Salon, Henrichement and Arrêt d'Ivoy-le-Pré (formerly known as Moulin Girard).'

And it so happened that he came to travel that line quite often, for in the summer holidays of 1903 his parents were posted back from Epineuil to Henri's birth-place La Chapelle. In fact it was a time of general bustle: Fournier's seventeenth birthday marked not only his parents' move to La Chapelle, but his own arrival at the great Parisian lycée of Lakanal, where he was to prepare for the entrance exam to the École Normale Supérieure. His parents, modest *instituteurs*, now expected their son to take the baton from their hands and become a distinguished *professeur*. Despite the slight eccentricity of the Brest episode, there had been nothing yet to disillusion them. . .

Alain-Fournier
as
photographer
(1899-1902)

2 · *Lakanal and the two Yvonnes (1903-1905)*

Lakanal is a lycée set in a park, the leafy and historic park of Sceaux, laid out to the south of Paris by Le Nôtre himself. The original château, built for Colbert by Claude Perrault, passed into the hands of Louis XIV's favourite son, whose wife, the Duchesse de Maine, turned it into a brilliant centre of eighteenth century arts and letters.

Lakanal today is a co-educational lycée, its green lawns and rustic paths swarming with boys and girls in casual clothes, giving it the rather appropriate look of a château en fête, recalling perhaps the 'Fête Étrange' of the novel. This is not to say that the attractive throng have ever read *Le Grand Meaulnes* or are even aware that the author passed that way. Yet the place in some way seems in harmony with Fournier. Living in such sylvan surroundings, he must have felt himself to be still in the country.

Fournier's class at Lakanal — the strangely named *khâgne* — had one sole purpose: to prepare students for the extremely competitive entrance exam to the Ecole Normale Supérieure, the great school in the rue d'Ulm, Paris. The professors were single-minded in their aim to get their charges past the winning post, but Fournier's misfortune was to join the *khâgne* at a time when his personal interests were broadening dangerously. How could he funnel those bursting energies down narrow scholastic paths? There had been a time when he was a model student, but not any more. History, for instance, was now a vital examination subject which completely eluded him, as did its professor, Paul Meuriot. The same could be said of Prof. Henri Bernès and his efforts to inculcate Latin and Greek. The professor of French, Francisque Vial, struck a chord only when he talked of contemporary French poets. (Three years earlier Vial had announced to his class: 'Gentlemen, M. Jean

Giraudoux is the only one among you who can write French'
— but no such crumb of comfort was thrown to Henri.) The
philosophy teacher, Camille Mélinand, did influence Fournier
considerably — he was the only one.

It was soon after his arrival that Henri met Jacques Rivière,
the man who was to become his best friend, but it was no
instant friendship. As Jacques later told André Gide, 'For our
first year together at Lakanal we did nothing but fight. He
mocked me endlessly and on any pretext.'

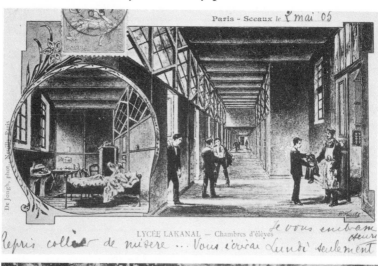

LYCÉE LAKANAL. — Chambres d'élèves

3. - LYCÉE LAKANAL. - Leçon d'Epée

Jacques Rivière was the son of a distinguished obstetric sur-
geon of Bordeaux. His family was in the high bourgeois tradition, made familiar to outsiders by the powerful novels of
François Mauriac. Dr Courrèges and his son in *Le Désert de
l'Amour* may not have been much like the Rivières, but the
background of that novel is exactly right. South-west France
before the First World War was a place of long brooding sum-
mers and stifling domesticity. The atmosphere at home was
such that even the loyal Jacques found it oppressive. Moreover,
he had lost his mother at an early age and now far preferred
the company of his maternal grandparents and aunts at Cenon
(on the eastern outskirts) to that of his father and stepmother
inside the city. The family was wealthy, but Jacques always
declined more than the minimum support.

In his introduction to *Miracles*, a posthumous collection of
Fournier's short pieces, Rivière has given a good picture of his
friend during that first year at Lakanal:

He himself possessed the same spirit of independence that
he later gave to Meaulnes. He had decided to demolish once
and for all the whole venerable and stupid institution of the
khâgne, an hierarchical organization governing the relationship between students, with special regard to the rituals and
humiliating duties imposed on the younger ones, known as
bizuths. He had placed himself at the head of a group of
rebels, with whom I secretly sympathized but could not yet
bring myself to join because of my timidity and my wish
to avoid distractions [. . .] I felt a little scandalized and a
little frightened, yet at the same time attracted to his personality. I hesitated to approach him and it was he who made
the advances, mixed though they were with much mockery
and teasing. It was clear that I irritated him, yet in some
way he was drawn to me. I was at the time methodical,
scrupulous, meticulous, and all that part of my character
made Henri extremely impatient. He played tricks on me
that I didn't always take very well. How many times, after
a break, did I return to my desk to find it turned upside
down, with books scattered everywhere – Fournier had
passed that way! At such moments I hated him with all my
heart but, as I said, he was at least showing an interest in
me, and slowly I became conscious of his sincerity, which
won me over and broke down my resistance. Then it was

Jacques Rivière.

that I found, alongside his indiscipline, a quite different aspect of his personality, which little by little revealed itself to me, and which I could love. Beneath that untamed exterior I found someone tender, naive, full of dreams and gentleness: in short, someone who, in the battle of life, was even more vulnerable, if that were possible, than I was.

Meanwhile Isabelle was incarcerated in the Lycée de Jeunes Filles de Moulin, where the girls were not allowed to receive letters from men, even if the men were their brothers. Henri's letters, therefore, had to be sent via Isabelle's local *correspondant*, who would smuggle them in during visits, making the whole operation much more exciting. Usually the letters hardly rated this cloak-and-dagger treatment, containing only the odd pithy paragraph on life back home, such as: 'M. Racottet, who faced the Prussians at Gravelotte, now faces Mme Racottet, supported only by a glass of brandy and *Le Petit Journal*.' But soon the letters begin to break new ground and, after describing how a Lakanal magpie wakes him from his dreams, and the leaves of Lakanal trees come floating down to rest in his wash basin, he goes on to report thrilling journeys to Paris, and 'walking down the Boulevard Saint-Michel in complete freedom'. Then Isabelle receives even more interesting news: the Wright brothers have just taken off for their first flight on Kitty Hawk beach, and Henri, too, has taken off. . . for his first love-affair. Isabelle described it emphatically as 'nothing serious' (*Images*, p.190) but perhaps younger sisters aren't told everything.

It was during the train journeys from Bourg-la-Reine to Paris in October 1903 that Henri first saw Yvonne G. . . He soon noticed that they were getting off at the same Latin Quarter stop near the Luxembourg Gardens and one day, when the pretty, dark girl was accompanied by a friend, Henri began following them. As they approached the Panthéon, which is situated on an island of its own, he doubled back round the other side and, just as they were noting his disappearance, advanced towards them head-on. Emerging thus from behind the monument almost magically, he swept off his hat and greeted them as old friends. The pick-up was impeccable.

There followed eighteen months of going to concerts and theatres together. Whether they became lovers is less certain, but they did exchange a vast correspondence. Well known at the Taverne du Panthéon, on the corner of the Boul' Mich' and rue Soufflot, they also chose to meet sometimes at the church of Saint-Nicolas-du-Chardonnet, down by the Place Maubert, because Yvonne went to lectures nearby. He even rented a room, but this (we are told) was only to change from his school uniform into clothes more suitable for the Sunday concerts. It was, precisely, Room 14 at the Hôtel Welcome, 5 Impasse Royer-Collard, just round the corner from the Luxembourg station: the hotel still flourishes.

Yvonne was somewhat older than Henri, as all the women he was drawn to tended to be. One of the most attractive things about her, in Henri's eyes, was that she came from the Cher, despite which she committed the gaffe at their first meeting of calling Epineuil a one-horse village. This he forgave her and they soon became close and oblivious to the world. For them the great event of 1904 was not the signing of the Entente Cordiale but the interception by Mme Fournier of a series of letters sent by Yvonne to Henri at La Chapelle. Writing to Jacques on 17 August 1904, Henri reports: 'For the last fortnight life here hasn't been worth living. I'm treated as a kind of stranger in the house, though not positively disliked.' He refers to Yvonne cautiously, in code, as 'Yves' in the masculine. The climax came when he promised his parents to cut out his visits to Paris. He reported this to Yvonne, suggesting that he only intended partly to keep the promise. But Yvonne replied histrionically, 'You must keep the promise entirely, your future comes before me. . .', while carefully leaving the letter open for Mme Fournier to read. The whole thing gave Henri and Jacques an excuse to commiserate together on the duplicity of women.

Despite this, the affair continued for another year or so and, when it finally ran out of steam in the spring of 1905, it was due to Henri's jealous pique about another of Yvonne's men friends. He decided she was frivolous and had no soul, a criticism he was to make fairly regularly about other young women. In the meantime he asked for the return of thirty letters, some of which ran to fifteen pages. He even threatened to report the matter to her father, a station-master in the Paris region, if she did not do as he asked. But he never got them back, and they all seem to have disappeared except for one published by Jean Loize in his excellent biography. Addressed to Yvonne-Henri-13, their poste restante number at Bureau 25, rue Danton, on Tuesday 11 April 1905, it reads in part:

> I was so needing you last night and, sure enough, you guessed it [. . .] Still scented and tired from the dancing, you sat down and wrote that it was really me you loved, that it was really me you'd like to have been with, and that the

fragrance of your hair and the gaiety of your heart belonged to me alone. Merci, ma chérie [. . .] On the day of our very first meeting you told me so simply, 'Maman thinks I'm mad to like the rain.' From that moment I could imagine all your dreams and memories and sweet sadness: I guessed them and I felt them because when one's in love one knows everything [. . .] It would be too crazily and impossibly cruel if you didn't come on Sunday. So do come. You're so good, you gave me that good surprise and I love you. Can I expect something on Thursday too?

Although the affair was almost at an end, this Yvonne – whom we will call the *first* Yvonne to distinguish her from another more famous *second* – somehow kept turning up. Exasperated by her, he once made the amusingly sententious remark:

Women are so quick to serve up shared memories. Looking back I am unable to recall the least trace of snow that morning on the roof of the Cluny museum. But I was probably thinking of other things.

Almost instantly the mood changes from lively to evanescent, from Ovidian to Dantesque. There could hardly be a greater contrast between the two Yvonnes. That is why it is essential to give the *first* her proper place in the story, if only to bring out the full flavour of her successor: the lady who came to be identified with the Yvonne de Galais of the novel and the great spiritual experience of his life. For the strangeness of this second encounter was not at all what one would expect from the schoolboy Henri Fournier. Up till then he had behaved with women like any other student of his day. With the second Yvonne everything was different. . .

On the afternoon of Ascension Day, 1 June 1905, he emerged from the Salon de la Nationale at the Grand Palais, off the Champs-Elysées. Standing at the top of a flight of shallow steps he noticed a couple just below him: a tall blonde girl and an old lady. They were engaged in animated conversation, the old lady laughing at what the girl was telling her. As Henri watched, the girl turned towards him and gave him a long, cool gaze.

At length the pair wandered off. He followed them. The

girl was elegantly dressed in the fashion of that year: there were pink roses perched on her wide hat, bows on her black shoes. Her ankles, when visible, were so fine they looked as if they might snap. Her svelte figure and unbelievably small waist were half hidden by a loose brown coat, and she carried a white parasol. She had a habit of slightly biting her lip, and her eyes were of a still, unchanging blue.

He followed the women along the Cours-la-Reine where, some yards before the Pont de la Concorde, they boarded one of the river-boats. He too, boarded the boat, watching them discreetly as it moved upstream. The girl was not unconscious of his presence: as they alighted (at the Pont de Sully at the end of the Ile Saint-Louis) he could almost have touched her. And still he followed. In the Boulevard Saint-Germain the girl stopped to look at something that children had chalked on the pavement, turning once more to look at him. The pair finally disappeared under the *porte-cochère* of a house on that same Boulevard Saint-Germain. It was at the Place Maubert end, near the church where he used to meet the first Yvonne but – curiously enough – it has never been identified, even in the family. In the novel itself it became a two-storey residence (*LGM*, p. 159) which seems to suggest one of the side-streets rather than the Boulevard itself.

Back at the lycée Fournier made some urgent notes about the incident. From now on he made notes all the time. And on every possible occasion (Saturdays, Sundays, Thursday afternoons) he returned to the mysterious house on the Boulevard Saint-Germain.

On Saturday 10 June,, during a dramatic thunderstorm, he looked up at the house through the leafy trees along the pavement. At a first-floor window, curtained with white lace, he saw his vision again, 'dressed in black, a book in her hand, as she parted the curtain, saw me and smiled'.

The following day (Whit Sunday) he donned his school uniform – so as to appear honestly his age – and took up position at an early hour. While pretending to be a casual stroller outside her house he happened to glance across the street and saw her on the opposite pavement: she had been out for a walk and was now returning. For a moment he lost sight of her behind a group of people, then suddenly she had crossed the road and was advancing quickly towards him. He had just

Henri in his Lakanal uniform, 1905

time to murmur – as she brushed past him with her feather boa: 'You are beautiful'.

She disappeared indoors and, when she came out again, he followed her to the tram. On the way their eyes met and she half smiled. Climbing up the steps ahead of him, she caught her long brown skirt on the platform (a common enough occurrence with the sweeping skirts of La Belle Epoque) and, pulling it free, caused a slight tear. She alighted at the Place Saint-Germain-des-Prés, where he spoke to her again:

'Tell me that you forgive. . .'

'Sir, do you mind!'

She entered the church. He followed her to the Lady Chapel behind the main altar. After Mass he again spoke:

'Is that really your last word?'

There was a despairing look in her blue eyes as she replied:

'What's the use? I don't live in Paris. I'm leaving tomorrow.'

She moved off to the tramway office, and was waiting for the tram when he tried again:

'I ought not to follow you. . .'

'I've told you already. What's the use?'

And as she said the French words 'À quoi bon?' she raised her head slightly on the stammered b-b-b. He nodded despondently, then moved away, but returned. He began to speak quickly and humbly, defending himself and trying to explain.

Half turned away from him, she none the less listened. She let a tram go by, then another. Slowly they began to walk down the boulevard towards the river. And now they were talking quite naturally, like old friends who had recognized each other at last. They reached the Chambre des Députés but still carried on. He asked her name:

'I am Mademoiselle Yvonne de Quiévrecourt.'

She told him she was from Toulon, her father a naval officer. They had almost crossed the Pont des Invalides, reaching a point 250 yards from where he had first seen her — the magic circle had almost been joined — when quickly she took leave of him and asked him not to follow her. 'We are two children', she said, as if suddenly alarmed by what had happened. Retracing her steps across the bridge, she looked back twice, however, the second time remaining quite still for a few moments. Then she disappeared.

Mlle de Quiévrecourt was a woman of a type he was not used to meeting. She belonged to the upper bourgeoisie and had been educated at the famous Couvent du Sacré-Coeur, a building that once belonged (like Sceaux) to the Duchesse de Maine and later became the Musée Rodin (and home of Rilke). Jean Cocteau also lived there — in what had been the nuns' music room. At nights he used to see a light burning behind a corner window and only later learned it was Rilke's. It was perhaps a trifle unusual for a young commoner, in 1905, to approach — in the street, unintroduced — a lady with a particle to her name. But how was he to know? And what did it matter? What was so epoch-making about this encounter? The answer is: its remarkable effect on Fournier. He made little attempt to meet Mlle de Quiévrecourt again but, instead, allowed her to become an ever-present obsession which remained with him for *eight* years. When friends expressed surprise, Fournier would say simply: 'It was a great shared love, and words were said.'

It would take a psychoanalayst to do justice to the matter, but an early reading of Fromentin's *Dominique* may have had something to do with it. In that novel the hero meets the love of his life while still a schoolboy. She marries another but he is content to yearn. They both yearn for the rest of their lives. It is one of the many forerunners of *Brief Encounter*.

Also involved was Maeterlinck's *Pelléas et Mélisande*, and inevitably Debussy's music, which in those days had swept most of the young men of Paris off their feet. His first words to her ('Vous êtes belle') come from Act 1, Scene 1 — as does the line 'Je ne suis pas d'ici', which Fournier was later to use more than once about himself. Yvonne's 'Nous sommes deux enfants' is adapted from an idea in Act 111. The incident in which her dress gets caught and torn is to be found in Act 1V, Scene 3 ('Ma robe s'est accrochée aux clous de la porte. Voyez, elle est déchirée.') To cap it all he later told his sister that he'd hoped Yvonne, when asked her name, would answer 'Mélisande'. (We are back to Act 1, Scene 1.)

Maeterlinck   Debussy

There is a certain staged quality about the whole incident. Was Fournier already shaping history into art in the way that he reported it to others and even recorded it for himself? No doubt it is true (as told) to his emotions, but what relation does it have to the facts?

Whatever the answer may be, the portrait of Yvonne in the novel (*LGM*, pp.75-85) remains exactly as it is in his notes of 1905. The meetings on the Cours-la-Reine and Boulevard Saint-Germain are telescoped and transposed to a country estate in the Cher (the Chateau de Loroy), but Yvonne is still the tall, blue-eyed daughter of a naval officer. She still bites her lip as she gazes into the distance. She still has the small features, tiny waist and slim ankles. Her wardrobe has not changed: the rose-trimmed hat, the loose brown coat and white parasol. The dialogue is identical. 'You are beautiful,' says Meaulnes. And when he apologizes for importuning her, 'I forgive you,' says Yvonne. When she tells him her name, Meaulnes replies 'The name I imagined for you was even more beautiful.' 'What's the use?' asks Yvonne. 'We're two children, please don't try to follow me.'

But how near was the woman of the notes and the novel to the real-life Yvonne de Quiévrecourt? To what extent did he turn her into the *princesse lointaine* of Symbolist folklore? It is interesting to learn from Jean Bastaire, who saw a photograph of her, that — far from being some insipid pre-Raphaelite maiden or a pale Ophelia gliding on the waters of dream — the real-life Yvonne de Galais had a ravishing little round head and an almost gourmand look.[1] In fact, not evanescent at all.

[1] Jean Bastaire: *Alain-Fournier ou l'Anti-Rimbaud* (1978) pp.17-18.

3 · *Turnham Green (1905)*

Fournier decided to spend the summer holidays in London to perfect his English, so a job was arranged for him with Sanderson's, the wallpaper people, at Turnham Green. (Part of the old buildings are still visible in Barley Mow Passage.) The deal was fixed by the ever resourceful M. Bernard, the man who knew everybody. Henri would work in the export department, translating letters, and would live with the company secretary, Mr J. J. Nightingale, a 38-year-old, tweedy, fair-haired, pipe-smoking North Countryman.

England had always been for Henri the land of adventure. He hadn't forgotten those prize books at Epineuil and had only to imagine Robinson Crusoe 'standing at the basket-makers' (*LGM* p. 21) for his imagination to soar. Already he was thrilled, in the train from Newhaven on 3 July, by the countryside: 'the fields and trees all so green.' At Victoria he was met by a most distinguished gentleman, who took him to Berners Street in an elegant vehicle with two huge wheels and the driver perched up behind, which Henri understood to be called a 'handsome (sic) cab'. Almost at once he was whisked off to the Nightingales' semi-detached house at 5 Brandenburg (now Burlington) Road, Chiswick, from which, in the course of the next few days, he wrote home in ecstasy:

> My little room is on the second floor of a villa lost in greenery
> (. . .) Vaguely from downstairs I hear the lawn being watered; and vaguely I hear Missiz N who, like all Englishwomen, spends her time at the piano. Now and then a train whistles on the way to Richmond. . .
> The suburban streets are like country roads, lined with châteaux of Sologne that touch one another. . .
> When an Englishman smells a lime tree, he stops immediately, takes a deep breath and exclaims, 'Oh, lovely!'

But after a honeymoon period he began to have some slight

fears, one of which was that he would starve to death. On 9 July he wrote home:

> I must really tell you about the food, which is unbelievable. One has the impression all the time of sitting down to eat with big children, who, having for a treat been allowed to choose their own meals, have turned them into dolls' tea-parties. First they set out a collection of little knives, little plates, little forks and little cups, but never any bread – except on a tiny plate to the left where you find a thin buttered slice of a kind of brioche, and this you are allowed to nibble from time to time.

On 13 July he wrote again, this time in his apprentice English:

> My dear, will you kindly send, at the same time as the dictionary, the rolls you have offered me [. . .] Send so that my host cannot be displeased by seeing the contents. I kiss and thank you very much. Henry. I was very astonished by hearing of 14 July. I had quite forgotten. Good 14 July!

On 16 July, his stomach still rumbling, he took a walk 'to Trafalgar Square, Shaftesbury Road, etc' and there bought a French *petit pain*, which he ate in the street before the horrified gaze of the English who are so careful (he says) to hide themselves when they eat. And on 18 July there was a heart-felt thank-you: 'The rolls – smelling of dictionary, insufficiently cooked and a bit stale – were delicious.'

But on 25 July there came a final *cri du coeur*. Mme Fournier's son was 'literally dying of hunger': 'Mrs Nightingale has a way of asking "Do you wish another cake more?" with the emphasis on the "Do you wish?" as if to say: "You must not wish, you have enough."'

He had no objection at all, however, to English tea which (he declared) warms the brain: 'In Mr Naïghtineguèle's house we drink tea mixed with milk. It is an excellent drink which I can recommend.' Later he recommended it even to Jacques, making it sound like some exotic drug: 'The only thing to make me feel myself again is tea – divine tea, which raises the temperature and restores memory, conjuring old pictures to calm you and beautiful ones to excite you.'

Another institution he found delightful was the one that manifested itself every Sunday on Turnham Green: the al fresco religious meeting of the Chiswick Baptist Church:

It is a sort of wandering church to catch the people who are too poor or too wicked to visit the real church. The singers are mainly women, helped by some men and a few children, while the passers-by can stop and join in if they wish. When the hymns stop, one of the men stands up, looking a bit bedraggled and, for three-quarters of an hour with his hat on, delivers an open-air sermon. The onlookers don't react in any way, even though it is a terrifying sermon, which I can understand from beginning to end because he shouts it, rather slowly, in the old, simple language of the Bible. 'How shall we escape?' he shouts. 'How shall we escape if we neglect the great Salvation? How shall we escape?' And then he compares us successively to men asleep in a burning house and in a sinking boat. Powerful stuff, and all at the top of his voice. And the passers-by who don't wish to stop just pass on as if nothing were the matter. [. . .] I shall do it for you when I come home, and you will like it. It is still ringing in my head. 'How shall we escape?'

Fournier's admiration also extended to his host Mr Nightingale, but less so to Mrs Nightingale and her two offspring: Clara, or 'Clarrie' aged twelve, and a younger girl, who, like so many English Nightingales of the time, was called Florence. He was, in fact, in two minds about English women. He told Jacques:

I can't get used to them [. . .] it's the way they dress: too comfortably and too skimpily and the colours too light. It took me a long time to figure out what puzzles me most about them and then I realized that not one wears a corset, which gives them a loose, floppy look. That and the eternal bicycle and a boyish nose-in-the-air stance.

In a long letter dated 23 July 1905 to Jacques in Paris he devoted a whole section to what he called The Feminine Sex, which he found vastly different in England from what it was in France:

Let me tell you about one small adventure with one small English girl: it's sweetly amusing and nothing more [. . .] In the room where I work – for about ten minutes every hour – I have facing me (across a wide desk littered with dictionaries, huge ledgers and typewriters) three girls. And behind me, on the other side of a glass partition, there's an army of clerks doing sums [. . .] Two of the girls are splendid creatures with remarkable figures, who spend the whole time looking for a chance to flirt. They are certainly fine girls but not my type, and I don't want to get involved with them and the clerks, so (despite constant peals of laughter) I maintain a stony silence and that otherwise occupied look of a gentleman whose thoughts are far, far away. But the third girl happens to be the one who was first detailed to show me around and whom I at once summed up as: nice eyes and no body (it just doesn't exist), nineteen but looks twenty-three, with a funny little face [. . .] I noticed, too, that, though shy and reserved, she made great efforts to be amiable [. . .] So one night about six, when she was struggling to get her tiny arms round the big ledgers, I gallantly jumped up and in a twinkling bundled everything into the safe – for which I received a thank-you, a smile and a blush.

Well, a couple of days ago, I noticed that Miss N. took to school sundry pots of flowers. They were having a flower-show, like everyone else in London at the moment. There was to be a garden-party all afternoon and evening, at which the little girls were to sell ices. Miss N. invited me to come and buy one from her, but jokingly I asked her the price and told her it was too much, while Mr Nightingale, pretending to be me, announced more politely, 'Afraid I have to be elsewhere, Miss.'

After tea, about seven, I'd completely forgotten about Miss N. and had no intention of going to her fête. Instead, I went out to post a letter. I knew vaguely that her school was connected with a church, and that the whole thing more or less happened in church, but I had no idea where it was. However, on my way to the letter-box, I saw this little courtyard leading to a sort of church, which was illuminated. A programme was posted up outside, which I stopped to read because these days I'm always glad to learn new words. I had just got to a bit about 'strolling at leisure in the illuminated garden' when Mr and Mrs N. strolled up themselves. Mr N. had a word with me and I was just moving on to the post when Mrs N. begged me to stay and see her daughter receive a prize.

I went into the little garden and at first I saw only the

bushes hung with fairy-lights. But then I saw banks of flowers ranged along the walls of the bizarre little church, whose
stained-glass windows were glowing dimly. Groups of
young people came into my vision, and they included the
dashing girls from my office. Farther on was another group
of quieter, more serious girls. One of them detached herself.
She was quaintly got up in a strange little Directoire hat.
After first nodding to the N. family she held her hand
straight out to me: it was my office friend. So there we were,
the two of us, making heroic efforts to understand each
other – and, to my own surprise, succeeding.

It was clear that she had made a big effort to come and
speak to me, and the English words I heard her say have
since fixed themselves on my mind with the special life they
had that evening. I can still hear the way she said *should* to
denote obligation rather than the merely conditional, as in
'you should have come earlier.'

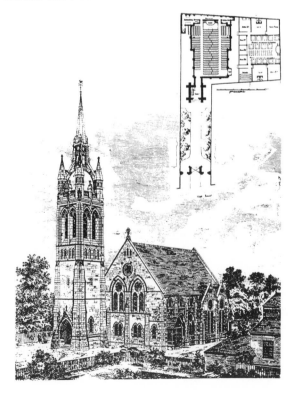

The small-talk we two exchanged concerned minuscule things, such as can only be discussed beneath a small Directoire hat with someone whose English is strictly limited. 'I go to this church every Sunday, that's why I'm here now. Tomorrow I leave for my holiday, but ten days is too little, isn't it? – 'But whatever shall I do without you?' – 'Oh really, for you the work isn't difficult, is it?' Like all English women she makes enormous use of the gentle 'is it?' and 'isn't it?' which turn the phrase into a question [. . .]
I stayed there for almost an hour enjoying a special kind of pleasure which I described to myself, perhaps because of the church and hat, as 'methodist'. Then I left her with a shake of the hand and a phrase which I believe is exchanged formally between gentlemen but which seemed to express my feeliing exactly: 'I am so happy to have met you.' And I strolled off home, alone but not in the least sad. . .

Though Fournier did not bring his camera to England, the next best thing occurred: during the preparations for this book, a small cache of unpublished postcards came to light, all sent by him from London. Scribbled across in his own brand of English – people with good taste were 'tasty' – these eighty-year-old views provide exactly the type of nostalgia which so delighted Henri himself. They introduce us to a lost world of hansom cabs and growlers, horse-buses and Edwardian bobbies, and at the same time we are poignantly reminded that the commentator who signposts 'Here is a policeman' etc was himself an Edwardian.

Those were the days when local events were apt to become postcards at the drop of a hat, so we find that the scene sent home on 13 July (on the card asking for the rolls) was of Turnham Green and a certain 'cricket-party before the factory'. The fading sepia enables one barely to pick out the players and, in the background, a row of lime trees can just be seen against the church. Those lime trees ('Oh, lovely!') have today reached the level of the steeple and, though the Sanderson factory has long since departed, cricket is still played on the green.

The card he sends home on 18 July (with heartfelt thanks for the *petits pains*) was of Grove Park, Chiswick. To come upon this little scene today, where so little has changed – where the Grove Park pub and the letter-box are precisely where he

"It is curious enough" that I have, this afternoon, only forgotten the first reason be-cause I was afraid (not sure, but only afraid) to be short of money: the great feast of the factory is on Saturday evening and night. It consists in an enormous flower-show, garden-party and ball — and I am afraid — but only afraid — to have some expenses to do. So, please let me have the order before Saturday night, if possible. I thank you, very very much — and kiss you in the same way I went last evening and night, by chance and only chance, with Mr. and Mrs. Nightingale to the place by my last post, and in card "Grove Park" that I did not know when I send some avenues around — it is, in my life, a — you delightful "unforgetable" walk — I kiss you Henri

The Houses of Parliament & Westminster Hall
London

Les petits pains qui sentaient le
dictionnaire, qui n'étaient pas cuits,
et qui n'étaient plus frais
étaient délicieux.

H. Fournier

Grove Park, Chiswick.

7071 The "Wyndham" Series

4/8 03 — 2ʰ 40 — I beg to acknowledge you — the
receipt of one letter, with accompaniment
of the report-card and of one house —

Henri

a policeman →   ← "a handsome"

(... ᵈ ᵉ National Gallery)
Trafalgar Square, London.

... elle le petit sœur - je regrette beaucoup de ne pouvoir t'écrire j'avais des foules de choses à ... te raconter et qq unes (j'une surtout) - ...

t'envoyer. ça sera pour fin Septembre - C'est bien loin London

De la maison, écris-moi souvent, je suis si seul ici.

Peux-tu soit le jour de ton départ soit en passant à Bourges me faire le plaisir d'envoyer une ou deux cartes postales de la localité jolies et originales s..

1° à Miss Clarie Nightingale - 5 Brandenburgh Rd. Gunnersbury. London. W. avec qq. chose comme: Isabelle Fournier envoie ses meilleurs amitiés à mademoiselle ...

2° à Miss Lilian Weber. 114 - Chesterfield Rd. St Andrews Park. Bristol avec q Pour l'album de Miss Lilian de la part d'H.F. avec les ... tu seras ... bienquittes ...

28/7/05

I'm in receipt of a letter from you which obliged me to spend one evening in the utmost parts of London. Thank you, all the same -

But I shall be very angry, if I have not, before Sunday morning, any answer to all what I have sent you - Yours heartily Henry

I'm sorry this p. card cannot give you an idea of all the gardens on the right hand; all the gardens & all the flowers around the palace

127

HOLLOWAY CASTLE.

Mr. Henri Fournier.
at Mr. Nightingale's
5. Brandenburgh Rd.
vous
J'écrivais Chiswick. London
England

Tu ne regrette ni Lakanal, ni ... vous soyez bien gentils

Bientôt au jeune Rivière - sans en attendre ...

left them – is strangely moving. A 20 July card to his father
(it shows the Houses of Parliament) goes into more detail about
Grove Park 'and the avenues around', which must have
included Burlington Lane and Chiswick House: it was (he
says) 'in my life a delightful, unforgettable walk'. Retracing
that walk, one can well believe it, for even today the district
can show sylvan glades like Staveley Road holding out bravely
against the traffic horrors of Hogarth Roundabout.

That 20 July card, incidentally, was among the mail he was
taking to the post on the evening when the Nightingales
waylaid him and enticed him into their daughter's garden-
party. It contained, among other things, a plea to his father
for cash, which he needed for 'the great feast of the factory. . .
an enormous flower-show, garden-party and ball' to be held
on 22 July. Organized by Sanderson's themselves, this second
garden-party of the week was (as he suggests) a truly grand
affair, quite out-classing Clarrie's. Here again he met a girl
wearing a small Directoire hat – it seems to have been the
fashion in Chiswick that year. Actually it had nothing to do
with Methodists: what he was observing was the tail-end of
the Kate Greenaway style, which had so delighted his fellow-
countryman Jules Laforgue some years earlier. The peaked
bonnet with the high crown and funnel back, tied with strings
under the chin, was still being worn by teenage girls in 1905.
What is more important, both girls with the distinctive hats
went straight into Fournier's novel (*LGM*, p 69), which he
was even then preparing to write.

It is fair to say that more than just the hats went into his
book. Much of the atmosphere of Clara's garden-party itself
seems to be echoed in the section of *Le Grand Meaulnes* in
which the children are staging 'La Fête Étrange' for the young
master of the mysterious domain. And, as if in corroboration,
the *Chiswick Times* of 21 July 1905 describes the fête at Gunnersbury Congregational Church the previous day as 'a flower
show in which the principal part was taken by the children'.

Did the music and colour of a warm summer night in West
London crystallize into the dream-like winter episode of 'La
Fête Étrange'? As it happens, Fournier's church survived until
quite recently (at 345a Chiswick High Road) but there was
little enough magic about the place. Fifty yards back from the
main road it stood abandoned, windows smashed, surrounded

by wasteland. Now only the car-park of a modern block marks
the spot. Could it ever have had the glamour that Fournier's
imagination gave to it? Perhaps the answer is to be found in
something he wrote later: 'In England I drew from myself,
and from nowhere else, some rather touching poetry.'

In his letter home after the big Sanderson garden-party Henri
reported that the women were obliged to run two strange races.
One involved doing a sum and the other threading a needle.
He suggested that 'it would never occur to anyone in France
to make ladies flap about in such an ungainly fashion'. Alas,
the *Chiswick Times* reveals that the lady who came romping
home first in both these races was Mrs N. herself.

Later on, when the Nightingales went off on their holidays,
leaving him to fend alone, he was dismayed to find himself
charged full-board for meals he did not have. But even then
he entirely absolved Mr Nightingale, putting the blame on his
wife: 'It's the lady!' (C'est la dame! si gentille qu'elle veuille
se faire, elle est bien déplaisante.') (*Bulletin des Amis*, No 22,
p. 72.)

If Fournier's feelings about Englishwomen were mixed, he
was also having trouble with one particular Frenchwoman.
His request to the first Yvonne to send back his letters having
been calmly ignored, he sent her a terse postcard which was
also ignored. Now Jacques sent ominous word that 'Yvonne
will be writing to ask you one or two questions'. Fournier
replied staunchly that he was well rid of someone who had
blighted his life for two whole years, making him 'the most
wretched and saddest of the sad'. But when Yvonne finally
decided to visit England and beard him in his den, it was too
late: Fournier was on his way home.

Toward the end of his stay he began, as usual, to become
nostalgic. On 14 August he told his parents: 'I admire and love
so many of the English characteristics: the natural reserve and
correctness, sobriety in speech and dress, a rich interior life.
Indeed, I can, in some respects claim joyfully to be an
Englishman.' And on 4 September:

As for England, I realize now that I've loved it all along
[. . .] Now, on the point of leaving, I'm already wondering
when I shall return, like Gide to his Algeria [. . .] Nothing
will stop my craving for their tea, which warms the brain,

and when I'm back home, you'll see, I'll love everything English twice as much. Being destined to become a schoolteacher, I shall regard it as part of my life, ever more deeply.

But he had not forgotten his other loves. Far from neglecting his beloved Cher, he had talked about it eloquently in a letter to Jacques and had even sent a postcard to Marie-Rose, his cousin in Nançay. To Jacques he said:

All my memories of that countryside return when I am deprived of it. Take La Chapelle d'Angillon, for instance, where I've spent the holidays for eighteen years: I see it now as the land of my dreams, from which I am exiled. I see the house of my grandparents, as it was when my grandfather was still alive: with the cupboard smells, and the creaking door, the low garden-wall lined with flower pots, the voices of the peasants, and so many other details that it would take pages to describe. [. . .] I even think lovingly of the food smells: the bread at lunchtime, the country cheese at 4 p.m. and my grandmother's cherry brandy.

Another land of my dreams is the one where I always spent a week or fortnight at the start of the shooting season. That's where I'd like to be buried; till now I've only had the joy of living there. I feel, rising within me at this moment, all the immense poetry (without exaggeration) of my life – of life as it is lived down there. It is my father's country, where everyone calls him 'Guste' or 'Toi'. (His name is Auguste.) You reach it after a dozen or so miles of travelling on abandoned roads in ancient vehicles. It's a country lost in the Sologne: the roads are dry and covered with pine-needles from the surrounding woods. The air is full of horse-flies, the roads often blocked by game. They're always having trouble with collapsed carts and sudden downpours, and horses getting stuck in the river while drinking. And, with all that, there are endless views at every turn, across the scrub and rough tracks to the horizon, views you probably wouldn't get even at sea, even at Toulon.

The final word was used as a kind of talisman: a coded reference that kept cropping up in the oddest circumstances, as when he gently reprimanded his sister, 'I asked you the other day for some information – I wanted to check something somebody said about Toulon. . .' (*Bulletin des Amis*, No 22, 60).

Fournier's farewell to these shores (he never returned) was a moving affair, England and Mr Nightingale being co-existent in his mind. Those two noble entities, indeed, were even more difficult to abandon when he considered the load of 'little men with goatee beards and moustaches' – his description of his own compatriots – whom he was about to rejoin.

And when Sanderson's reported back to M. Bernard that it had been impossible not to like the young Frenchman because he was 'such a gentleman', Henri passed on the news to Jacques, adding: 'I had to smile'.

Self-portrait, 26 August 1905: the handkerchief was to soothe a headache, but it strangely anticipates the appearance of Frantz de Galais after his suicide attempt

'I can in some respects claim joyfully to be English': Fournier in his London hat, opposite page

At La Chapelle, 18 September 1905

4 · *Last year at Lakanal (1905-1906)*

Fournier now began his third and last year at Lakanal where, unhappily, he was to be deprived of the company of Jacques Rivière. Having failed his entrance exam to École Normale, Jacques had accepted a grant to study for the *licence* – something like a BA degree – in his native Bordeaux. The result of their separation was a period of intense letter-writing, during which they endlessly probed one another's characters.

Rivière was an acute critic, even at that age, and probably influenced Fournier more than the other way round. Quite early on he tackled the problem of Henri's *sensiblerie* – a tendency to sentimentality:

> There, I've said the dreaded word. I think you are moved a little too much by things that aren't worth while. I'm afraid, for instance, that your enormous admiration for *David Copperfield* and (Edmond de Goncourt's] *Germinie Lacerteux* is partly due to your liking for the false sentiment of little things. That anecdote of the assistant master [Mell] is nice enough in its way, but it's also – how shall I say? – mawkish. Those are things that, when they are true, are heart-breaking; but in a book they're just too much. Leafing through *Germinie* I notice quite a few things in that style. Universal pity is fine enough in its way, but you can't feel sorry for everything [. . .] I think you should be careful. Despite their talent, or even genius, Dickens and Goncourt and Daudet could well be dangerous for you: and I'm telling you this so that your book won't be just a banality. Let it be strange, contrived, false, devious or what you will – but, for the love of God, not banal.

To which Fournier replies (to summarize slightly):

> Yes, but all that is just semantics. Sentimentality is when it

doesn't come off – when it does, you get a true expression of life's sorrow. If you'd actually read *Germinie Lacerteux* instead of just leafing through, you'd know that a whole chapter is devoted to Mother Jupillon, the incarnation of sentimentality, simply to highlight the truth of Germinie herself. If you'd read *David Copperfield* you would have realized that I recounted that anecdote of the junior teacher in the baldest possible terms, precisely to show you how the sober art of Dickens can turn dross into gold.

Rivière sums up with a shrug of the shoulders:

Well, perhaps I shall never like either book unreservedly – it's a matter of temperament, and we disagree about irony [. . .] What I understand by irony is not to believe too much in anything and not to take life too seriously. Given that, I'm bound to believe that too much literary commiseration, if it isn't strongly based on reason, becomes sentimentality. It's only because I've been through this phase of universal compassion myself that I can now despise it – otherwise I wouldn't have the right to talk.

Rivière was feeling rather sorry for himself at this time: he had seen enough of Paris to fall in love with it, and now he was condemned to life in the provinces. His letters to Fournier tend to be strangely evocative for a man wedded to reason:

'Paris! How beautiful it is! I think of Rémy de Gourmont saying that the Quai Voltaire is one of the great landscapes of the world, and it's true. I can remember the evening I left, weeping on a bench in the Tuileries and thinking I might never return.

A day or two later Fournier takes up the refrain in his letter to his parents:

Have just had the saddest letter from Rivière. He won't be back for maybe three or four years, and Paris for him is the centre of the world. He's right. On Sunday I went to the Salon d'Automne from three to five, and came out just as the autumn night was descending. I took the boat from the Cours-la-Reine to the Chatelêt. The Seine was dotted with lanterns, with an immense grey backdrop behind the Eiffel Tower. The leaves in the Tuileries trembled in the evening air. Oh how I hate those provincial lawyers who look at Paris with the eyes of English tourists! When you've spent three years in Paris in your youth, as I did, you love it like the country, like views across fields. It's as precious as life itself, despite the sad, dirty corners. And even with all its provincial lawyers and English tourists, it is still a *salon* frequented by the most intelligent and cultivated people in the world. Forgive me, but I had to get that off my chest, and I could hardly say it to Rivière – it would have been too cruel.

Something had to be done about Jacques' plight: he would have to come back soon, if only for a few days at Christmas. So on Henri's suggestion he took a room at the Welcome, the hotel where Fournier used to change for his expeditions with the first Yvonne, and the visit itself is recounted in Henri's Boxing Day letter to Isabelle. He adopts a breathless style to amuse his sister. Something like this:

Saturday evening – Waiting at station. Rivière arrives with suitcase and cape, looking like Russian nihilist. We set out for Opera, discussing Wells, Kipling, etc. My first visit to Opera and nothing special. I return to Bernard's: Midnight, bell, door, blackness, matches, name for concierge, where stairs? up not down, key, door, kitchen, salami, thirsty, cold, blankets, sleep, angels.
Sunday – Meet Rivière. To Louvre. Lunch with Bernard. His stories. Every night during Commune he went to theatre to keep warm. Tells old, complaining servant: 'We'll have to find you a lover, Mrs Haps.' We walk to Champs-Elysées, where Rivière is to dine with family friends. The red glow over Paris, and car headlights beaming into sky. We discuss Schopenhauer, Leibniz. Hegel, Pascal, Renan and Barrès, walking too quickly to see anything but our thoughts. I go back chez Bernard, who's away celebrating Christmas Eve with some gay old souls like himself. Return of Rivière, who says: 'I nearly got run over, but at least in this town you *can* get run over.'
Christmas Day – Long conversation with Rivière about him, me, the world. Then to Théâtre-Français: a one-act play for little girls of twelve, followed by three acts by Hervieu fit for no one at all. Couldn't even snooze, the actors shout

too much. Return, staircase, candle, sleep, apotheosis, wake
up, cold, coat, gloves, station, train, letter, kisses, Henri,
the end.

A sketch of his friend Guéniffey,
in a letter to Isabelle

Fournier and Rivière often had cat-and-dog arguments, and
one such occurred at the beginning of 1906. Talking of Jacques'
recent Paris visit, Henri says:

> When I consider a small parcel of life that we lived together,
> I have to laugh because what is so clearly revealed is the
> divergence of our two personalities. For you our Christmas
> meeting meant the clarification of certain ideas and the
> development of this or that theory. 'Fournier' for you meant
> someone to try them out on. (Of course, I'm exaggerating
> slightly.) But for me, the same holiday meant evenings of
> feverish life, when, in the bitter cold and under a sky, black,
> luminous and electric by turns, we hurled hundreds of
> words, ideas, theories at one another, uniquely to convince
> ourselves that we were alive and friends.

Fournier always resisted Rivière's tendency to categorize
him but the very need to resist enabled him to discover himself:

I have a horror of the classics, and hallowed taste, phrases one repeats without thinking, poetry without life in it. . .
I believe that all life is worth living. When we evaluate life, despising one kind and glorifying another, we are fitting it into a scheme of things, an ideal world, which has no more reason to exist than some other, totally different, world or scheme. . .
Shall we ever know at what age in our life we come nearest to the truth? Couldn't it be that the vision of life we have at eight years old is superior to that which we have at thirty. . .
Neither philosophy nor art nor literature is worth the years of life lost studying it.

Fournier's most potent influence (after Jacques) was the Lakanal Professor of Philosophy, Camille Mélinand, whose governing philosophical idea was 'poetic intuition'. After the failure of philosophy, there is only intuition: to find the secret of the world, one should be in a state of inspired sympathy with it, the act of wonder being more valuable than reason. In his *Notions de philosophie* Mélinand wrote: 'Art creates (using material from the real world) an imaginary world. The child lives in just such an imaginary world, of which he is the author. Merely to exist, it is probably necessary to imagine reality other than it is.' Mélinand was the sort of teacher who could change people's lives with an off-the-cuff remark like 'Don't live a month longer without reading *Jude the Obscure* and *Tess of the D'Urbervilles*. But Fournier was capable of making his own discoveries, which around this time included a certain Colette Willy, whose *Claudine à l'école* he pronounced 'un chef d'oeuvre de naturel – Colette Willy a du génie'.
Meanwhile Isabelle was growing up – she would soon be seventeen – and on 7 February Fournier wrote her a long letter, embodying many of his most personal thoughts:

I'm happy you're working well, because I'm not. This exam means nothing to me. If I got a grant for the *licence* I'd have to sign a ten-year teaching contract and I just don't want to be part of the university. If I did better and got into École Normale I'd have to embark on an endless round of work for the *agrégation*, and I don't accept the idea of wearing out one's brain on that sort of thing. However, I'm quite happy because there's always 'life', to which I submit myself humbly and deliciously, while trying to express it in poetry and in prose. Life has nothing to do with studying for the *agrégation* till mental collapse supervenes.

The life that sweeps us along on its seas is unknowable. Reason is but one of its wretched playthings. Intellectual schemes may seek to dominate it, but they will be swept away. The wise thing is to renounce thought, abandon yourself to life, become part of it. Not for me those forms of words that are constructed, like card-castles, over the river of life. The only words I respect are those that seek to express life in its true complexity.

My book may be called *Gens du Domaine*, or anything else so long as it suggests the kind of life which intimately involves my personal thoughts – and when I say thoughts I mean dreams and memory more than reason. Mind you, I don't like the word *dream* too much either. You know the sort of people who call their books *On Wings of dream*, which is enough to put off ordinary mortals. They seem to be saying, 'Hey, look at me. I deal in art, beauty, dreams and that sort of thing. So buzz off the rest of you.'

This was a dig at Bernès, the Classics master at Lakanal, who in his youth had perpetrated just such a book (*L'Aile du Rêve*), of which Fournier said, 'Its lack of success was so complete that the mere memory of it still poisons his timid existence.' (*Bulletin des Amis* No. 22, 60.)

And finally he left his sister with a memory she could share:

This morning my window's open wide and in front of it there's a wall. On the other side of the wall there's an avenue of tall trees which belong, I'm told, to the Marquise de Trévise, having once belonged to the Duchesse de Maine. At least, that's what they tell me, but all I know for certain is that early this morning there reached me from over there a great freshness, with some birdsong and a memory: the rather feverish beginning of a summer's day, later to become very hot. We'd loaded the parcels of prize books (all beautifully done up) on a wheelbarrow, and were taking them, you and I, to the teacher. . .

Isabelle Fournier, aged 16

His letters to Rivière were in a similar vein:

> I feel as if I were full of crushed desires. Coming down from
> my cubicle just now, I looked out of the staircase window
> and saw, behind a wall, a château, looking just like a piece
> of scenery let down from the sky. There was a shady alley,
> a gate, a corner of park with moss at the base of each tree.
> I saw steps leading up to the entrance and shining wet tiles
> on the roof. Ah, these great desires of mine that crush them-
> selves against a window-pane. Over the years, in lycée after
> lycée, I've had my fill of them.

He reproves Rivière for not having taken (on the spur of
the moment) a job offered to him in Egypt – which he (Fournier) would have accepted like a shot. He toys with the thrill

of renouncing everything: 'Ah, to throw in a suitcase just one's papers and a change of linen! To say goodbye to everything one loves: La Chapelle d'Angillon, Épineuil, Nançay, the Cours-la-Reine, the Boulevard Saint-Germain!'

On 21 April he writes:

> I wasn't seeking to be happy – in this dull, suburban train which trundles through the April night – and yet I'm happy. I'm allowing everything to enter my soul, as in the distant days of childhood, when, driving through villages where the children were playing after supper, I let their whole world become me. I let it all enter my soul, without thinking of what was there already, just as I am doing now, in this dull train which trundles through the sweet night.

On the first of May a law was passed, allowing young men who reached the age of eighteen that year to volunteer immediately for a single year's military service, instead of waiting to be called up for the customary two. Rivière at once took advantage of the scheme and begged Fournier to do the same. But Henri was not in the least perturbed by the idea of military service, which he thought might be a useful, even enjoyable experience. To which Jacques retorted:

> If your love of the people really goes that far, I take off my hat to you. But, knowing you as I do, I think you'll live to regret it. I don't deny that army service brings some advantages, but they're bought at a terrible price.

It happened that Fournier at the moment was more concerned with other things, such as the first anniversary of his meeting with Yvonne de Quiévrecourt. On 24 May (Ascension Day) he duly retraced his steps of the previous year, from the Cours-la-Reine to the Boulevard Saint-Germain, and reported to Rivière: 'She wasn't there.' To which Jacques replied, perceptively but perhaps unwisely: 'Maybe your unhappiness on the anniversary day was really a kind of happiness – and perhaps you owed it to a happening in the past which was itself relatively unimportant.' More in sorrow than in anger, Fournier reproached his friend for 'the blasphemy of your letter'.

In the meantime, and without much surprise, Henri had failed the entrance exam to École Normale and, far from being offered the compensatory grant to study for the *licence*, lost even his grant to remain at Lakanal. 'It's all over, I had no luck,' he told Jacques on 7 June.

Half way through I developed sleeping sickness or something very like it. Dr Laffont stuffed me with glycerophosphates and caffeine, which had some effect but too late. In Latin composition the slightest difficulty made me doze off, so I just put down the first thing I thought of, making some incredible mistakes. In philosophy I decided quite simply that, if a certain student sitting in front of me turned round, I would hand in my paper blank. He didn't [. . .] but there were phrases I had to re-read twenty times without understanding them.

On 5 August he added, 'My marks were really morbid [. . .] I must have been semi-conscious half the time.' And from La Chapelle on 15 August there came this bewildered message: 'On my way down here after the exam there were moments when I asked myself: I'm in this train, moving through the sunny countryside, but where's it taking me? Am I about to be reborn?'

As if to deepen the wound, one of his friends at Lakanal whom he always referred to as 'little Bichet' had gone through to the École Normale with flying colours. 'My dear, *Je suis ravi de ton succès*,' wrote Fournier, and his Anglo-French congratulations were genuine. But he was never one to be too impressed by academic laurels, and Fournier, the dashing rebel, would always regard Bichet as the same shy, cautious, studious little swot – though lovable in a way. In fact, all Fournier's letters to Bichet were written in this same half-patronizing, half-affectionate tone of voice. And his advice to little Bichet, now as always, was: Who dares wins. Odd advice perhaps to come from the loser, but it is a measure of Fournier's basic self-confidence that, even at this low ebb, he still believed in his star.

For the long holiday at La Chapelle he brought down a paying guest, a colleague from Lakanal, originating from Panama, called Don Pedro d'Aguilera. This flamboyant playboy was just what Fournier needed after the horrors of June, for Aguilera had a way with him and soon delighted the whole family with his wonderful stories. There were descriptions of his mother's estate, where you could walk for thirty miles without seeing a house, where the forests were so dark you had to carry a lamp even in daytime, where boa-constrictors could eat tigers in one gulp. There were stories of the wars of independence that took place regularly every three years: Aguilera himself had been a lieutenant-colonel at seventeen and the most feared soldiers (he said) were little bare-chested boys of eight and ten. Fournier passed this all to Bichet, with some additional details reserved for Léon Bernard, the elder of his correspondant's two sons:

> Aguilera has a shirt in his trunk which has been pierced by a sword-thrust, and a hat riddled with bullets. He has that casual air that goes well with a dark complexion, and an urge to jump on every horse he meets. He's been a judge and will soon be an M.P., unless he's made Panamanian Minister to France. He wants to take my parents back to Panama, where foreign teachers earn fabulous salaries.

Regarding his own state of health Fournier tells Bernard: 'For a month or so the slightest mental exercise sent me into a fever but now, thanks to phosphorus and a period of rest, I manage to follow simple conversations.' To Rivière he suggests that the Cher itself has played the greatest part in his recovery:

> Just as the Goncourts apostrophized Paris, I'd like to do something similar for this country of mine. I'd say that, if I've been able, perhaps more than most, to avoid the worries, anguish and bewilderment of growing up, it's because I could always re-discover my true self at the gate in the corner of a field where they're harnessing a couple of horses to the harrow. And never has my countryside been more indulgent and sympathetic than now, in this year of moral drought, cooling my fever and healing my troubles, like lavender heals wounds.

And there seems to be hope in the message he sends to little Bichet on 20 September:

> I don't know any greater sensual delight than when I feel – in the most various and hostile circumstances – an unfamiliar memory that rises from the depths of my heart. At first it's complex and indistinct, some faint image from a former life.

'Little Bichet'

Sometimes it will continue to emerge, slowly losing that first complexity and strangeness. But at other times it remains where it is, deep down, crushing my heart. And that is more thrilling and strange than the greatest love. I'm collecting these moments. When I have enough of them – and that means when I have the time and strength to concentrate on them entirely – then perhaps I'll be able to express the inexpressible and it will be my kind of poetry.

It had also been Wordsworth's kind of poetry, as it would be Proust's. But Proust was luckier than all the others: It was he who finally found the key (the *madeleine*) which unlocked the door. He found the way back to childhood that Fournier spent his brief life looking for.

There were family deliberations that summer about Henri's future, and the note of disappointment can well be imagined. His parents, however, though ambitious for him, were not unreasonable. In the end they came up with a quite surprising plan. Henri and Isabelle would share a flat in Paris, and Maman-Barthe, the old maternal grandmother who had never left her native village, would keep house for them. Henri would have one more try at theÉcole Normale exam, this time working as a day-boy at the Latin Quarter lycée of Louis-le-Grand, in the rue Saint-Jacques. As for Isabelle, she also would attend a local lycée, the newly-opened Fénelon for girls.

If Henri had reservations about sitting a second time for the fateful examination, he kept them to himself.

5 · 60 Rue Mazarine
(1906-1907)

The idea of living all together in a Paris flat was more exciting than the reality. The bustling street outside, linking the river to the Boulevard Saint-Germain, may well have had its charm. But the flat itself was dark and poky – and the building full of strange smells and noises. Isabelle later called it 'our little black home in the rue Mazarine'. Situated between ground and first floors, the flat consisted of three cupboard-like rooms, plus a minute black kitchen in which Maman-Barthe nonetheless produced marvels. The windows gave on to a small square courtyard, occupied by a paper works whose horse-drawn vans thundered through the *porte-cochère* immediately beneath the flat.

Today the place has hardly changed. The rue Mazarine is, if possible, even more choked with traffic. The name of the firm in the courtyard is different. In Fournier's time it was the Papeteries du Pont-de-Claix (paper-makers); today it is the Librairie Grund (book-publishers). And the horses have departed.

On 11 October Fournier wrote to Rivière 'at about 5 p.m. by lamplight in my narrow, dark room'. He laments both the low ceiling and the dark courtyard, where not a leaf is to be seen, nor even the sky. His carpet is the colour of dead leaves, but the lamp warms his head slightly, which is presumably a bonus. As night falls the courtyard shutters begin to close and the babble of voices becomes less intrusive. Now it is raining and the room is so small he can shut the window without getting up. On 9 November he announces that most days he has been kept busy from six in the morning to eleven at night on lycée work. He is snatching time to write to Rivière:

I'm free till 2.30. A horse has just come into the courtyard.

It's the beginning of a November afternoon, which will get darker and darker, and only the caged canaries sing. Perhaps at this very moment Catherine Martin [a girl he knew at Epineuil] is letting her sheep out on to the frosty road.

He now considers it a crime to have uprooted Maman-Barthe and to have brought her to Paris. Her old chest-of-drawers looks so out of place; and even her pendulum clock which so pleased him in the country, strikes a false note here. Yet life still has the odd good moment: one of his rare delights is to see Isabelle going off to read Laforgue in the Luxembourg and, 'This weekend, in my little room, I've squeezed tremendous joy just from my *freedom*.'

To little Bichet he appealed:

Any ideas for the mural decorations of a poor student's lodging? [. . .] The address is 60 rue Mazarine, a lively thoroughfare; the room's on the mezzanine floor, dark but mine own: a sort of chapel, the colour of dead leaves, in which I exist pitifully and suffer from the lack of living leaves. My head, which a little regular work had steadied, is now spinning again with fever. At first, Louis-le-Grand hoped they had found a master of composition, a skilled translator and a fine essayist, but now I'm in disgrace again, just as I was at Lakanal. I shall never be a Normalien.

It is true that the terrible regime to which all French students are subjected was taking its toll again of Fournier; and it was a relief when the Christmas holidays came round and he could retire to La Chapelle. As he told Jacques, 'That twice-daily walk to the lycée, and prison for the rest of the time, did me no good. I missed the fresh air and green leaves of Lakanal.' But this was not the season for fresh leaves, even at La Chapelle: 'When I went down into the garden this morning, two crows rose from the field and came down farther on. Winter is here, like in those old advertisements for Chocolat Poulain'. To Isabelle and Maman-Barthe ('*Mes chers enfants*'), who had remained in Paris, he reports on the parents' new maid, who 'used to be a shepherdess and has a curly top to prove it. Like the sheep, she's also rather slow and deaf but she doesn't say Baa – she says 'Hê-ptigas!' and a *petit gars* (small boy) arrives'. To Isabelle again on New Year's Eve he announces:

In a corner of the schoolyard we sculpted the most primitive snowman: in style he somewhat resembled those old Celtic idols, with a touch of Neptune as to the beard and haircut. Yesterday, at six o'clock his head fell off, and today he's a pile of slush. As Laforgue said, 'The gods depart.'

Isabelle had been to see *Julius Caesar* at the Théâtre Antoine, and Fournier comments:

I think what's so fine about Shakespeare, that man of the north, is his free-and-easy way with pompous plots: the manner in which he rewrites scenes from the depths of his dark and precise imagination. What a nightmare, for instance, what an anguished Hamletic dream, he makes of Brutus battling with his indecision! And how beautifully un-Latin it all is! [. . .] Shakespeare imagined an English Rome, whereas our set designers of 1906 have given him a genuine southern town, drenched in sunshine and complete with noisy and boastful throng, a sort of Marseilles that has decided to be the centre of the world [. . .] Well, it's nice to see classical heroes brought closer to us, but bad luck for anyone who'd rather see the original Shakespearean nightmare.

While working and overworking for his exam he never lost sight of the book. Jacques continued to receive hesitating and vague messages like the following:

My credo in art and literature is childhood: the aim thoroughly to explore those mysterious regions, my hope to maintain a perpetual to-and-fro between dream and reality. By dream I understand that vast and imprecise life of the child, which floats above ordinary life while all the time receiving from it echoes and reminders [. . .] Delicious and half-known things happened to me, leaving behind only the impression of delight; yet somehow the delight has to be expressed.

But the bulk of the correspondence between Jacques and Henri was of a literary and ephemeral nature. The two young Frenchmen had a vast appetite for new authors, most of them soon forgotten, but for whom they would willingly have died at the time. The poet Francis Jammes was an early favourite – a natural enough choice for Henri Fournier: in such books

as *De l'Angelus de l'aube à l'Angelus du soir* (1898) Jammes
wrote simply of the everyday joys of country life, exactly as
Fournier knew them at Épineuil during the same period. But
later the poetry of Jammes lost its charm. Hundreds of pages
were then covered with argument and counter-argument about
Maurice Barrès. At length they discovered the great Catholic
writer Paul Claudel – and later put that particular genie back
into the bottle, though not before he had delighted them with
La Jeune Fille Violaine.

Francis Jammes

Paul Claudel

A significant date in their literary and artistic progress was 16 December 1906, when Jacques (from Bordeaux) told Henri, '*J'ai vu Frizeau*'. Gabriel Frizeau was a celebrated collector who knew everyone: not merely Jammes and Claudel, but younger men such as the painter André Lhote. His house was full of treasures, Gide first editions and canvases by Gauguin. It is typical that, on his very first visit there, Jacques met a disturbing young man who persisted in remaining silent and, in the days that followed, 'haunted and intrigued' him. Rivière was irritated by the almost insolent refusal of this very young man to react in any way to the overtures of the kindly Frizeau. This strange youth, with the shut-off manner and unconscious impertinence, turned into the legendary poet and diplomat Alexis Saint-Léger Léger, better known as the Nobel Prize winner Saint-John Perse.

'Rivière is on the point of meeting everyone we most admire,' wrote Henri to little Bichet. Already, earlier in the year, Rivière had been reading André Gide with delight: 'Wonderful man!' he tells Henri on 7 August. Before long, thanks to Frizeau and the young Lhote, Jacques was actually to meet the great man, and his whole life be changed.

Fournier's own incursions into the literary world of Paris at this time were rather different and much less inspiring. At the Café Vachette, near the Cluny museum, his first encounter with Jean Moréas (a Greek poet, né Papadiamantopoulos) was sour to say the least. Their second meeting (on the first floor of the Deux-Magots, Place Saint-Germain-des-Prés) was disastrous. Moréas had been holding forth in a pompous manner about Jules Laforgue, whereupon Fournier jumped on a chair and pointed an accusing finger. Perhaps he quoted Laforgue's famous insult: 'You and I, Moréas, can never co-exist.' Had the Greek been a shade less amorphous a duel might have ensued.

All this while, to the puzzlement of his friends, Fournier maintained his posture of adoration towards Yvonne de Quiévrecourt with constant, if cryptic, references. At the beginning of 1907 he told Jacques that his new name for her was 'Aimée Mince', which he preferred in its English version of 'Amy Slim'. In the same letter he mentions that

the belfry of Saint-Germain-des-Prés stands out against the sky like that of a village church lit by the moon. Unknown shadows have come here in search of the night and of silence. Someone weeps. I have entered here only once since the Great Adventure.

And in the very next paragraph he says this:

Not long ago I met the *first* Yvonne. I wasn't prepared for it but I was superb: I behaved as if she were a casual school-friend, of whom one asks politely, 'Have you been well? and how was England?' And then goodbye. After all, that's

Jean Moréas

André Gide

Jules Laforgue

better than a lot of unpleasantness and, seek as I may, I can't find any reason for regret. Just for a moment [Thomas] Hardy had me worried: what might he have thought of me? But the affair, after all, only amounted to a few kisses. The whole idyll happened inside me, only inside me.

But if Jacques considered that the same might be said of the Mlle Quiévrecourt idyll, he did not again risk saying so.

Fournier's letters are an excellent barometer of his state of mind and health, and the one dated 17 March is especially revealing:

The other night I came into my room and saw a beam of light, which I took to be moonlight. But it was only a lamp in the flat opposite. One lives in a maze of streets, courtyards (. . .] The other day I felt so fine in my black felt hat, quite the elegant young man until (suddenly, in a shop mirror) I saw a peasant, solemn and shaved up to the nines, on his way to some wedding or funeral. . .
I'm conscious of all that I can't achieve. I know that my whole life is only a *desire* for life. I know that one day I

Self-portrait by André Lhote, 1908

shall know landscapes, moments and women that will give me the feeling of 'setting forth' – that swelling of the heart you get when you leave on a long journey. A journey towards happiness? No. Because one is pretty certain not to arrive, at least not in the right country [. . .] Yet that swelling of the heart as you leave is almost better than arriving, more precious than happiness.

Still doing his military service, Rivière must have smiled at that last remark: he had lately been on guard duty at Bordeaux station, and had watched with eager excitement the trains leaving for Paris.

What keeps me going is the thought of that admirable month we'll spend together when I'm liberated. The minute I'm free I'll dash to Paris. Yesterday I had a vision of the Paris countryside, with all those exquisite names on the stations: Etampes, Angerville, Savigny. I already felt the train jumping – and the colder, fresher air coming in the window.

Earlier he had written: 'Paris still wrings my heart. I trembled the other day as I remembered the noise the carriages make on the asphalt at night, and the dull toc-toc of the horses.'

Fournier, having been to La Chapelle for Easter, had himself just returned to Paris:

I came back on a gentle, rainy afternoon, with a swelling of the heart impossible to describe: the great thoroughfares are already green, the streets as animated and profoundly mysterious as when, a country boy, I first set eyes on them. Summer in Paris is like nowhere else: gentle rain on the boulevard leaves, the clear bells of the trams that endlessly pass [. . .] Come and see the trams.

There was no room for Rivière at 60 rue Mazarine, at least not to stay, but he was invited to eat every meal there. Fournier told him about Maman-Barthe and what was special about her:

For me she's still the Maman-Barthe of my childhood, of the holidays, someone quite legendary. Today she's only a poor old lady, very hard-working and childlike, on whom a discipline of silence and painful discretion has been imposed. Maman-Barthe awaits you, with potato soup at lunch and dinner for those who like it.

After first suggesting their old place, the Welcome, Henri finally booked his friend into the Hotel Cluny-Square, 21 Boulevard Saint-Michel – where the Boul' Mich' crosses Boulevard Saint-Germain. This was probably then, as now, one of the most hideously noisy spots in Paris – but the room on the fourth floor was light and cheerful, with a splendid view across the Cluny museum to the Panthéon. Best of all, it was only five minutes from the Fourniers' flat.

Little is known about the month of May 1907, which Jacques spent in Paris at the end of his military service. (The sad thing for biographers is that when their characters meet, they no longer write letters to each other.) All that is known for certain about these four weeks is that Fournier's sister Isabelle and his best friend Jacques fell in love.

But did not for the moment tell Fournier.

With Jacques back in Bordeaux, Henri sat a second time for the entrance to École Normale. He was judged admissible on the written part, which made his subsequent failure in the oral all the more disastrous. He was again refused a grant for the *licence*, and now it was clearly the end. He thrashed around, wondering what to do next. He even tried to join the Chinese Customs Service, which was at that time run by the British. Even then he had not plumbed the depths of his despair, for on Thursday night, 25 July, he wrote to Jacques: 'To top everything else, listen to what I've just learnt: Mlle de Quiévrecourt is married!' In the letter which followed he explained how one of his friends had come round to the flat on the evening of the exam result and, to cheer him up, had sung him a song. It didn't help that this was Verlaine's poem 'Mandoline' (from *Fêtes Galantes*) in the Debussy setting, which had the instant effect of reducing Fournier to tears. But, after drying his eyes, he rushed round to the house on the Boulevard Saint-Germain and did what it had never occurred to him to do before: he walked in and asked the concierge for news. Quite simply the concierge told him that the young lady on the first floor had married last October and was living at Versailles as Mme Brochet. Fournier was shattered.

Understanding him better than most people, Jacques quickly decided to get Henri away to Bordeaux for a holiday. He needed to deploy all his wiles, including the promise of shoot-

ing stars over the Garonne ('*Il y aura des étoiles filantes*') before
Henri would accept. But that August with the Fermaud clan
at Cenon was a holiday he wouldn't forget.

The Domaine de Saint-Victor, as it was called, housed a
crazy commune made up of Jacques' maternal grandparents,
aunts and uncles, great-aunts and great-uncles, as well as his
sister and two brothers. They were a highly conservative
group, sticklers for etiquette and tradition, but this did not
stop them indulging themselves with the latest novelty – which
this year happened to be motoring. Even Jacques had caught
the bug and had written to Henri:

> The other evening I came back alone with the chauffeur.
> We crossed the centre of Bordeaux at speed, lightly brushing
> the pedestrians on our way. I shuddered slightly and the
> chauffeur, noticing it, remarked in a passionate and madly
> lucid aside, 'Say what you like, I could kill the lot of them
> if I wanted to.' I was terribly moved, it expressed so perfectly
> the sheer spiritual exaltation of power.

Jacques' uncles did not go so far as their young chauffeur, but
they sometimes achieved quite considerable speeds. The full
flavour of life at Cenon comes out in some of Henri's letters
home:

> The house is a little like Mme Benoist's at Epineuil, but
> wider and taller with a tower. The residents are charming
> too. Up till now we've mostly been out cycling, but yester-
> day we watched the big automobile race. In fact we passed
> the doomed car only minutes before the crash, and we pre-
> dicted aloud what was bound to follow. We went back in
> the evening to see the two crushed vehicles: it was terrible.
> You'll have noticed I forgot my shoes. Could you send
> them, please?

He was enjoying the experience of living in an enormous
family, where everyone had his nickname – from Jacques'
younger brother Marc ('Kim' or 'Mowgli') to his little sister
('Princesse' or 'Mousmée'). The rather grand house was on
top of a hill, with a view of Bordeaux to the west. The garden
ran half way down the hill, stretching from acacias and yews
at the top to vines and peaches below. Even the different parts
of the garden had their nicknames: it was an in-family with

The Rivières' house, near Bordeaux

in-jokes but full of kindness. 'Between excursions we spend the time reading or playing dangerous games.' His first automobile ride took place on 4 August 1907 – the date is recorded, just as the date of his first aeroplane flight was, five years later, on 28 June 1912. He regales his friend Jean Bernard with more mad memories of motoring:

> We only hit the occasional obstruction: a doorway, cat or maybe pedestrian. Despite the lust for speed that seizes us, and despite epic contests between the small car built for racing and the big eight-seater crammed with mothers and fathers, there has been only one fatality: a dog that got itself caught between wheel and engine. Took us two hours to repair. Glorious as Kipling!

It will be noticed that, being a French boy, his 'sentimentality' did not extend to animals, and the perils of motoring (he confides to Jean) have at least taken his mind off other things, such as love in the person of Mme Brochet. And at the end of the glorious fortnight he wrote home:

> I return to you with my eyes full of sun and my legs full of kilometers. Dazzled by the luminous seascapes of France and Spain, and after implacably fine weather for all our excursions, we woke this morning to rain. Time to leave.

From La Chapelle he wrote a thank-you note:

> Just to say that I am back in my own countryside, the private one that can only be seen by pulling back branches. On the way it was raining and I've never known it so fresh and hidden. I wish you'd been with me when Bourges Cathedral emerged from the meadows and poplars [. . .] I won't forget Aunts Emilie and Marie asking me to name my dearest wish – so they could pray for me, poor dears, at Lourdes.

The preparations now began in earnest for Jacques' reciprocal visit to the sacred land of Fournier. Fussing around nervously, Henri finally decided that Jacques must enter his kingdom by train, for the railroad best suggests a journey into the unknown. On a bicycle one glides into a village by a road that later becomes familiar, but by train one is suddenly there as if by magic. 'The walks I'm planning will help us to lose ourselves,' he says confidently, the aim being to feel that villages only twenty miles away are on the confines of the known world. It is almost as if he is arranging the set for *Le Grand Meaulnes*: 'This morning at six I heard a threshing machine. One day we'll set off with no plans at all except to find it.' He recalls a childhood memory of that moment before the train draws up at La Chapelle, just as they passed the castle, when his mother used to say, 'Look at me, darling,' and remove a speck of soot from his face with her handkerchief. Jacques is then moved to dream of his own mother, long since dead: 'She touched me on the neck; it was here by the drawing-room windows. She wore a blue dress.' Henri reciprocates with a recent story of his father:

> I got up at 4.30 and went off with him fishing. The sun was rising, and the village was bright and clean and empty, like

a stage-set before the curtain goes up. But every so often –
in that white, sleeping village – a solitary man would emerge,
all ready for work in the fields, and set off in his own chosen
direction. The steps would die away, and then another man
would appear and go off in another direction. And it was
impossible to guess where the next man would come
from. . .

Rivière's month at La Chapelle was a fitting sequel to Fournier's cure at Cenon. To Henri's delight his friend fell in love
with the quiet Cher countryside and, when he returned to
Bordeaux, enjoyed it still more in memory, according to the
well-known Fournier formula.

As Jacques explained, he found himself talking very little
about the Cher to his relations, except to make vague general
remarks about the large number of woods to be encountered,
or the plethora of streams. He would allow himself, at a pinch,
to converse about Bourges or local archaeology or to say, for
instance, 'In Sologne, at this time of year, the game is most
plentiful.' The rest – everything that mattered – he was hoard-
ing up for himself.

The two friends had never been closer: though Isabelle was
with them, she had yet to come between them. She and Jacques
were still keeping their love a secret. . .

6 · *Military servitude (1907-1909)*

Fournier now faced the ordeal about which he had been so light-hearted a year before: his two years' military service. At the beginning of October he joined the cavalry barracks at Vincennes and sent the regulation jokey postcards home. The one for Maman-Barthe showed a dragoon in the act of writing on a wall: 'Only. . . days to go!' The figure to be written in by the sender of the card was in this case a formidable 741. To Rivière he announced simply that 'Henri Fournier, of the 23rd Regiment of Dragoons, regrets he is unable to attend this year's Salon d'Automne.'

Three days later the joking had to stop: in a letter dated 5 October he told Rivière:

I confess I'm in a ghastly state of depression. This morning I went back to the doctors in the hope of being rejected for military service altogether. That's not possible, so I'm asking M. Bernard to have me transferred to the infantry.

The ever-obliging M. Bernard arranged this promptly: a month later Henri had become an infantryman at the Caserne des Invalides. Needless to say, he immediately regretted the change:

Vincennes was a château compared to this! My companions there – from the Berry and Touraine – were handsome, clean and intelligent compared to the little Normans here with their harsh and unintelligible speech. They're drunk and stinking, the lot of them, their faces lined with dirt, their heads raw with scabies and ringworm. Last Wednesday, when I got in at midnight, I was expecting that sour smell of the Vincennes barrack-room, a nasty enough mixture of respiration and button-polish; but here the air was unbreathable, suffocating. As I felt my way in the darkness, trying to find my bunk among all the others, I didn't know whether to go on or give up: all that sweat and filth and smoke still hanging about from the oil lamps, added to the breathing of 300 men in one room! Once in bed I discovered what I hadn't noticed before: four inches behind my head, another head sighed and snored, sniffled and groaned, breathed and belched. At least at Vincennes, if you woke in the night, you could lie and think – but waking here in the night is torture. For four days my immediate neighbour was a syphilitic waiting to go into hospital. He insisted on using my mug, with the result that I just stopped having coffee. In the same way, all one's belongings are filched and swapped around, so that you drink from another man's mug, or wear his cap, without even knowing it.

Ironically it was in these circumstances that Fournier received the proofs of his first published article, a rather prim piece called 'Le Corps de la femme', which he had written for Jacques Rouché's *Grand Revue,* as a reply to what he considered the crude sensuality of Pierre Louÿs. It was the first time he used the pseudonym 'Alain-Fournier', with its faint echoes of Alain-Chartier, the poet of Agincourt and author of *La Belle dame sans merci.* Fournier had chosen the name to distinguish himself from another, already famous, Henri Fournier, a racing driver whose exploits were often celebrated in the press. There had been the occasion, for instance, of the great race at Bologna when 'Henri Fournier, flashing past the stand at 170 km an hour, drew gasps of admiration and horror as he crashed at the Borgo bend.' But when the magazine finally appeared on the bookstalls on Christmas Day, the proud author was slightly deflated to see himself described on the yellow cover as 'Allain Fournier' – two l's and no hyphen.

One of Fournier's first duties at the new barracks was to teach some of his illiterate and scrofulous companions how to read and write. Surprisingly, it was a duty that gave him some satisfaction since, unlike most of his other occupations at the time, it seemed to have a point. Another mitigating circumstance was the closeness of the barracks to his Paris home, making it possible for him to go back to the rue Mazarine for the evening meal and at weekends. Jacques was now in Paris, looking for teaching work, so the two friends often met. From 2 December Jacques and Isabelle considered themselves engaged, but still in secret – and on 29 December Aguilera, of Panama, took everybody to see Réjane in Sardou's *Madame Sans-Gêne.* Earlier they had been to an adaptation of *Sherlock Holmès* at the Théâtre Antoine. Fournier wore for these occasions the infantryman's red trousers and crew cut. The latter, he told Rivière, debarred him from all thoughts of love ('Je suis hors de l'amour'). 'Even the wretched kid who's been pursuing me for the last three years would be cured forever if she could see me now.' It was his last reference to the first Yvonne.

After a series of route marches by night in the south-west suburbs of Paris, Fournier was put on guard duty at the Chambre des Députés, a moment in his life which should cer-

tainly have been recorded for posterity – indeed it would have
been if Mrs Nightingale, then in Paris, had remembered to
bring her camera with her. Henri was introduced to the latest
'Night' (his word for a small Nightingale) but the only person
he cared about was missing: *Mr* Nightingale, of whom he had
said, 'Like many Englishmen, he is a poet without knowing it.'

But suddenly there was news of real importance: Fournier's
parents, the dedicated country schoolteachers, had been
rewarded at last with a transfer to Paris. They had been wanting
this for months, but it was still traumatic when it came: the
end of pike-fishing for M. Fournier, no more village socials
for Madame. The aim of the move was to keep the family
together, and it was M. Bernard's ultimate triumph. Henri
wanted it too, since it would give him a firm Paris base, to
come back to after his military service. As for Isabelle, she
was not sorry to be released from the daytime gloom of 60 rue
Mazarine.

A new and larger flat was needed, and it was found almost
at once in the next street. A minute's stroll down the Passage
Dauphine led them to 24 rue Dauphine, which was certainly
a move in the direction of light and spaciousness, if not a very
great one. The Fourniers still looked from mezzanine windows
into a courtyard, but it was a larger courtyard. Maman-Barthe,
her noble work now done, could retire again to La Chapelle,
to be visited for the holidays. Before leaving she was given
two treats: she was taken to see her grandson on guard duty
outside the nearby Senate; and, a few days later, she attended
the official engagement party of her granddaughter.

This event delighted everyone except Henri, who, quite
unreasonably, felt betrayed: as if his best friend and his old
confidante had ganged up against him. Jacques once more
understood the trouble: during the next few months he made
every effort to comfort the disconsolate soldier by keeping
him in touch with all the latest Paris happenings, such as the
wonderful production of Musorgsky's *Boris Godunov* at the
Opera, heralding the imminent arrival of the Russian Ballet;
or the latest book by Gide, to whom Jacques now felt closer
'than to any other living writer'. Fournier, for his part,
acknowledged the indispensable nature of their friendship,
come what may:

Jacques gives life to ideas, while I deal in things and moments and people [. . .] Yet the person who has helped me most to approach my own special dream-world is Jacques Rivière with his immaculate theories and so-called abstractions.

Corporal Fournier and his men: Mailly, 15 June 1908

Henri was now promoted corporal and moved to the Fort de Vanves, a barracks in the south-west corner of Paris and not by any means his favourite posting – though it is here, curiously, that the city of Paris has chosen to honour him with a Square Alain-Fournier which takes some finding.

In May he marched his men all the way to the great camp of Mailly, between Reims and Troyes: the first step in his exploration of France at the Government's expense. As Jacques has written, 'He discovered France step by step,' – from Champagne to Touraine and from Laval to the Pyrenees. In the course of it he also learnt – unlikely as that must have seemed at the beginning – to love the men he served with. 'They were debating the other day,' he told the family, 'as to whether perhaps I wasn't even better than the best corporal they'd ever had. I mention it because it's all I have to be proud of at the moment.' To Jacques he recited the names of some of these men: 'Marolle, Feuillant, Fauvel, Reyne, Bellanger', and added, 'They're all as ugly as their names are beautiful.' It's true that he claimed to recognize, in one hated sergeant-major, the features of Jarry's Père Ubu himself, but – come September when a number of the men left for home to become civilians again – he contemplated them with wonder. As free citizens, how different they looked! In their civvies you couldn't possibly mould them together and lead them *anywhere*. How could the big, smocked cattle-trader ever line up to obey an order with the canny little Breton peasant in his beret and embroidered waistcoat? 'They'd never arrive together at the same time.' Yet the uniform had made this strange thing possible.

Precisely at this time, a year before, he had observed veterans leaving Vincennes:

> There was a blacksmith, several peasants and a saddler. One man was called Fontaine, he was going to Guerche. Another to some village near Bordeaux, I forget the name. Both looked tough and happy. I desired nothing better than to go off home with them, on that rainy October day, which for me meant the end of everything but for them spelled the beginning of life renewed in the villages and farms of France. Next year, at the same time, I too shall be leaving: it is my favourite, the most admirable month of all.

To his father on 16 September he wrote: 'I'd like to be with you now – we'd go to Nançay.' And to Jacques on 27 September he could not resist recalling yet again Nançay in autumn:

> When I went to Nançay in the old days, I was determined to see it as a place of wonder, unique and mysterious [. . .] I remember waiting there for relations to arrive from distant parts, and how disappointed and disgusted I was when some too familiar aunt stepped down from her carriage, looked around with assurance and began holding forth in the way I'd heard a hundred times before. I felt that deep in that woman was the certainty that she had nothing more to learn about life: there was nothing new about her, nothing new she could ever bring to others. She considered that people like herself had learnt, once and for all, the truth about everything. How many women are there like that, who carry about with them, in their every expression and gesture the same miserable assurance! How sweet and desirable, on the

other hand, as she steps from her carriage in the evening, is the woman who is still thoughtful and mysterious, full of the world she has come from, yet with eyes uncertain and dazzled by the world she is stepping into!

The vision is almost of a Hardy heroine – say Tess of the D'Urbervilles; he had read the book the year before in response to the urgent invitation of Camille Mélinand.

Such was the spell of Nançay that, on the last day of the holidays there, he would go into a trance-like state, making his girl-cousins exclaim, 'We can't make out what's the matter with him – he's all misty-eyed.' ('*Il est tout mousse.*')

For little Bichet, too, in this favourite month of September, Fournier recalled the past – but in the shape of Mlle de Quiévrecourt:

I never saw anything so serious and childlike. She smiled once, but her eyes had a kind of well-bred despair, as unfathomable and blue as the sea on the plages of the Côte d'Argent and the Mediterranean, whence she came. She was haughty and proud, her first response to me being the disdain she doubtless reserved for all who approached her uninvited. She was not to be approached: she was the young lady with the white sunshade, who opens the gate by the château on sultry country afternoons.

He must have liked that image, for he returns to it in the same letter:

Why am I telling you all this? [. . .] to understand what I mean, you would need to have been a peasant child like me, who's waited endlessly on Thursday afternoons in June [. . .] by the great white gates that close off a private road, on the edge of the château woods.

This is magical ground for Fournier, recalling as it does the approach to the Domaine Mystérieux (*LGM*, p. 59): 'Au coin du bois débouchait, entre deux poteaux blancs, une allée où Meaulnes s'engagea.'

The autumn manoeuvres in Touraine that year left Fournier with another characteristic image: the memory of a thoughtful little girl in the courtyard of a house at Azay, where he and his men had gone to buy wine. She sat quietly at a table reading, oblivious to all the bustle around her. 'I have never had such an intense impression of two kinds of life: one, exterior and insignificant; the other, life as the little girl knew it.' On another occasion it was a small boy, watching at the door of his house as the regiment marched by – who turned to go in, then waited a few seconds more, to savour the pleasure while it lasted (*'comme pour s'appuyer sur ce peu de plaisir encore.'*). And another small boy, the son of a baker, who sat by the fire, head in hands, with his own special thoughts (*'Il suit son étrange pensée.'*). Fournier could 'identify' with these pensive children because he understood as few have done since Baudelaire, 'the green paradise of childhood loves' (*'le vert paradis des amours enfantines'*).

His second year of military service began with a move to Laval (150 miles west of Paris) in October 1908. He was now a sergeant, training to be an officer. It was here that Jacques sent news of a new periodical planned by Gide, called the *Nouvelle Revue Française*, to which Fournier gave his immediate blessing because 'I always dreamed of a review with "France" in the title.' Shortly after this Jacques actually *met* Gide (at a private view of André Lhote's pictures) and reported that the occasion had exceeded his wildest hopes (*'dépasse toute espérance'*). Gide, it transpired, had a noble head which resembled Baudelaire's. On arrival he had asked to be excused the connoisseur's customary exclamations of delight – but before leaving had promised Lhote a very practical introduction to the dealer Druet. And, to cap it all, Jacques had been invited to write for the *NRF*! To little Bichet, Fournier confessed that the mere mention of this fabulous event had thrown him into a decline, he felt so far away from the fount of all true joy. Training to be an officer – despite his 'exquisite new greatcoat with the velvet collar' – was not to be compared with meeting Gide. And to add to his frustration, he next received news of Rivière's first visit to the Gide house at Auteuil: 'I've never before,' said Jacques, 'had that feeling that, as we talked, the same thoughts were being born simultaneously in our two minds.'

For Christmas Fournier came to Paris for a few days and later

André Gide

recorded his impressions. They resemble those that T. S. Eliot evoked two years later in 'Rhapsody on a windy night' – and both writers show quite clearly the influence of *Bubu de Montparnasse*, the masterpiece of Gide's friend Charles-Louis Philippe:

> I look at Paris [says Fournier] with a love that is made up of horror and terror, as well as old intimacy. This is the poor creature who for years has been my companion – whose every gesture is familiar to me, even if I still can't guess what frightful secret the gesture conceals. Here at night are the lit corners of streets which I know so well, yet always see with the same dread. Here are the empty pavements, and the houses, like lines of boxes with their crannies and lanterns [. . .] Behind these walls that I can touch, a whole race of men – strangers – are sleeping.

One day he would try to do for Paris what he was doing for the Cher department:

> I'll find the real landscapes, with their living souls, that exist behind the sordid songs of Paris, which whores sing in the simplicity of their hearts. I'll find the landscapes that exist behind the painted *café-concert* decor: a world as terrible and mysterious in its way as the world of my other book.

Early in April he was sent, for the last six months of his military service, to the town of Mirande in south-west France. Here, if lucky, one is within sight of the Pyrenees – and indeed sometimes, between the clouds, Fournier saw the Pic du Midi, which looked 'like a sleeping camel'. Fairly soon he realized that he'd picked up the local accent – that was when he stopped noticing it in other people.

Today the Maison Hidalgo, the house where he lived, bears a plaque – and photographs from those days show a dashing second-lieutenant in his black tunic embroidered with gold. From a simple 'second-class' earning a sou a day, he had scaled the heights to corporal, sergeant, and now officer, at last to achieve a modicum of prosperity and leisure. He could enjoy a round of tennis parties with the other officers and their wives: 'Everyone's charming, and so am I. Some call me "tu"; others even "Henri". Nobody knows, of course, what goes on inside me, as I greet the tennis ladies in my unbearably correct and elegant fashion.' He finds the other officers mostly tedious; but the women, as always, more interesting:

> Take that rather ceremonious one that I was introduced to the other day: I knew at once that, a little later, lost in the throng, her anguished face would turn and seek me out. Or that other one, so impertinent in her black dress and Louis XV heels, I knew that at the end of the evening she'd come quietly to my side. That's why [Dostoevsky's] *The Idiot* moves me more than I can say. And that's why I practise towards women, Jacques, the delicate art you reproach me for. It's because, with women, the fragile exterior or maybe futile envelope allows you to see through and almost touch the soul. And it's with women that I'm conscious of having a soul myself.

To little Bichet he put it this way:

> Jacques reproached me the other day for my so-called purity: being too pure in my attitude towards women. But that's not the point at all. What I've always had for them is the look of *The Idiot*, which goes first to the soul. With women I can see the soul: I recognize it in the bend of a neck as the anguished face turns towards me; in the hesitant confession of the haughty, and the painful abandon of the ceremonious. They come to me, as to the innocent Prince himself, with a love that does not know itself by that name.

Years later, with his usual perception, Rivière had the last word:

> I can see now all that he discovered of himself in Laforgue [. . .] Like Laforgue he had a huge longing for women [. . .] but the union of souls had to come before the union of bodies: he needed love to be absolute. All the exigencies of Laforgue, Fournier recognized as his own, and he knew at the same time that such a dream was scarcely realizable.

In a letter to Bichet, Fournier went on to describe an incident with a certain Josepha, a discreet lady well known to the officers, whom she received with ceremonial liqueurs and conversation:

> At the most nocturnal hour of the spring night, I find myself in the house of the lost woman. I have slept in her bed, and

Sketch of Fournier by André Lhote

there is nothing more to be said. I am now about to leave by the stone steps into the garden, to slip away into the darkness. But just as our secret meeting is ending, she touches my arm and sinks back on the bed.

'Listen,' she says – and sure enough a voice rises near us in the garden, mounting with a joy that stirs us, with a purity to disinfect hell. The nightingale. And the woman smiles at me, like someone who has often seen angels gathered together in a certain field but never mentioned it – yet mentions it now, since you are crossing the field with her, to reassure you. 'He's there every night,' she says.

It was with such thoughts in mind that Fournier went to spend Whitsun at Bordeaux with the painter André Lhote. One of the pioneers of cubism, Lhote did not subsequently fulfil all his youthful promise. He is perhaps best remembered today as a remarkable critic, the *NRF*'s principal art pundit between the wars, and the man who revealed to the modern world the full glories of Egyptian tomb-painting.

> I told Lhote I thought his wife was beautiful. I was expecting some clever aesthete and I found this young ingenuous girl [. . .] On Sunday he led me across town to my bed in his fine palace of a studio. On the way he talked about love and he felt it was almost monstrous to be given such happiness. He described his dazzlement at their first awakening together in bright sunlight when she said, like a child, 'My eyes are stinging.'
> I talked to him about the soul of women, but for him it meant their virtues of abnegation and simplicity whereas, for me, the soul is like an endless valley which opens up before you. The movement of an arm, a look, an inflection of the voice, and you're impelled forwards towards a revelation, a communion, a departure. I've felt it for the least virtuous of women: more humbly perhaps but just as mysteriously as for the others. They've given me the longing for great unknown lands in the image of their souls.

Fournier now sent Jacques a prose-poem called 'Dans le tout petit jardin', and received in reply some excellent criticism. Rivière was never afraid to tell the truth as he saw it:

> I wonder if this is really the best you can do. In my opinion that letter to Bichet about the nightingale was a hundred times better. It seems to me that, for a great rebel who refuses to admire the classics, your work isn't as free as it could be. I am tempted to say what Lhote said of his 'Garden of love' painting: it's too careful. Without losing control, you should let the colours run across the outlines.

Jacques was probably also wondering just then how to break the news of another disappontment. Fournier had submitted to Gide a piece called 'La Partie de plaisir', which Gide claimed to have lost, though it seemed more likely that the mishap was a diplomatic one. When Jacques at last extracted a verdict from

the great man, it was brutal. 'This is not the moment,' said
Gide, 'for prose-poems.' In the event – when Jacques had
summoned up sufficient courage to pass it on – the cutting
criticism cut away dead wood and Fournier was grateful to
Gide for his frankness (though he could never bring himself
actually to like the man).

One of Fournier's seminal books for 1909 was certainly Dostoevsky's *The Idiot*, which he had begun reading at Laval and
continued to read throughout his stay at Mirande. In his strug-
gle to evoke what he called his 'strange lost paradises', he found
the book influencing him more and more, until he almost
reached the point of 'identifying' with Prince Myshkin, not
only in his own mind but in letters to his friends. 'Since
Claudel,' he told Jacques,

> no book has brought me closer to Christianity than *The
> Idiot*. The word is never actually mentioned; yet, reading
> the book I'm tempted to believe as never before. Perhaps it
> is the bridge I've been needing, to cross the gap between
> the Christian world and my own.

He was helped in his quest by another book, whose influence
on him was hardly less: this was the Bible, as translated by
Monsieur de Sacy (1613-84), which he had borrowed from the
chaplain of a hospice adjoining the Maison Hidalgo. Later he
found a big, leather-bound copy on the *quais* in Paris, which
became one of his most treasured possessions.

The book was a revelation to him both in content and style.
'I'm reading the Bible like an old Englishman', he told Jacques.
'The Apostles have an infinite glory and simplicty: they tell
everything, without embarrassment, because they saw it.'
With which Jacques concurred: 'The style we ought to use, if
only we were brave enough, would be something like St
Matthew's.' Henri agrees: 'Exactly! It's what Laforgue called
"Christ's French".'

After identifying with Dostoevsky's Russian Prince, there
were moments now when Fournier seemed almost to see himself as Monsieur de Sacy's Christ. So much so that his mother
became seriously alarmed, suspecting that it was all the fault
of Claudel, whom her son must be trying to emulate. It was
indeed a major religious crisis, aggravated by several extrane-

ous events, for example the death of Jean Chesneau, one of his friends at Lakanal. Chesneau had had the original idea, while still at school, of renting a room in the Latin Quarter (in Rilke's rue Toullier) to entertain his friends on their days off. The 'Thursdays of Toullier Street' were attended by, among others, Jean Giraudoux, who now offered an epitaph for Chesneau: 'He had the charming tolerance of those who know that nothing's worth while.'

Jean Giraudoux

And about this time, when his hero Blériot was successfully flying the Channel, Henri had a last fling at the *licence*, and crashed. While in Paris on that occasion he had constant rows with his family and later wrote:

> That was his greatest fault: the harm he did to those he loved caused him so much remorse and pity that he seemed as he made them suffer, to be torturing himself [. . .]
> He would load his mother or friend with such bitter reproaches that he himself would break down sobbing. At such times he would suffer remorse and still be pitiless.

It's when I feel most moved, when I'm brimming with affection, that I become especially hard and cruel. And the woman who becomes my wife, if she doesn't know me well enough, will often weep. [. . .] There's too much pride and dissatisfaction within me, which nothing will remove. Perhaps my soul takes up too much room inside me, ever to share space with another.

Finally there was the marriage of Jacques and Isabelle – attended by Henri in his elegant uniform, but not by Jacques' father, who had refused his blessing. By a coincidence which he found disturbing, the event was celebrated in the Lady Chapel of Saint-Germain-des-Prés, where, four years before, Henri had followed Yvonne de Quiévrecourt. After the ceremony, while the newly-weds were at Cenon, Henri wrote them some strange letters, half-fact, half-fantasy, but full of despair, which worried them.

At the end of his stay at Mirande, Henri had a brief, passionate affair with a girl called Laurence, whom he met in the public garden, sitting on a bench with her elder sister. He made a point of talking to the older girl to excuse the fact that it was the younger one who attracted him. But Laurence misunderstood and left. Some time later he found her again. It was of Laurence that he wrote:

> When men saw her slow smile, which began at the corners of her mouth and then blossomed like a kiss, even the most surly would become agreeable, just to see it again. And the shyest of men would dare to look her straight in the eyes so that, unable to resist the challenge, she would smile her slow smile. . .
> Ah, what a proud little girl she was! To see her standing there in her white shoes, one foot pointed in front of the other, you'd have sworn she was a tightrope-walker about to exercise her skill. Her hair was black and shiny, like that of the market women with their baskets. You couldn't help thinking of a young gypsy and, if someone in town happened to remark, 'Mlle Laurence is ill', you'd immediately think : 'The gypsy's ill. There'll be a light behind the red curtains of her caravan.'

The affair lasted hardly a month and its end, on a Sunday in September, is probably described in Fournier's short piece 'L'Amour cherche les lieux abandonnés' ('Love seeks deserted places'). The girl knows it is their last meeting together, but cries, 'Let's go on. Let's get lost.' And pressing her hair against his eyes, whispers (in the manner of Maeterlinck's Mélisande): 'Feel how damp it is!'

There was a further anxiety. Fournier was examining a report from a detective agency: it revealed to him (wrongly as it happens) that Yvonne de Quiévrecourt was now a mother. And on 21 September he wrote to Jacques: 'She is more lost to me now than if *She* were dead'. And the capital letter, of course, was Fournier's.

7 · *New faces, fresh fields (1910-1911)*

Fournier was twenty-three. His parents' hopes for him in the academic world had collapsed. What to do? His first answer was *sleep*: quite simply to get up as late as possible in the morning. And when he got up: to do nothing. All his life he had been doing things, albeit unsuccessfully; now he had an overwhelming desire to take it easy. He felt that at last he had been released from a long series of institutions, both educational and military. Since leaving the paradise of Epineuil he had been through eleven years of lycées and barracks. It was enough.

So the *rentrée* – the return to work – happened that year without Fournier. History does not record specifically if he got up, on the first of October, for the visit to the rue Dauphine of Paul Claudel. What we do know is that he extricated himself from the threat of that mighty steamroller, shaken but unconverted.

As it happened, 1910 turned out – not a year for taking things easy – but a year of great movement, when his life seemed to move purposefully forward at last. With hindsight, it is appropriate that one of his January letters to André Lhote gives the first mention of the name 'Meaulnes' as the hero of his book. In the course of the year the project which he always felt inside him began slowly to take shape, and he evolved a writing style to express it. Other developments were:

He met, and became friends with, the two living writers who most resembled him and most influenced him: Marguerite Audoux and Charles Péguy. . .

He experienced his most down-to-earth love affair to date: with the girl who was to become the 'Valentine' of his book. . .

The problem of how to earn a living resolved itself in a way that afterwards seemed inevitable: he became a journalist. . .

Finally, the Fourniers moved into a setting worthy of them: the calm and airy rue Cassini, in the Observatoire district of Paris, south of the Luxembourg Gardens.

All these developments overlapped in the untidy way that life ordains, so that it is difficult to plot them chronologically. It's true that in January he took his first step into journalism by approaching Jacques Rouché for a regular job: it was in the middle of February that he met Jeanne Bruneau, somewhere along the *quais*; and late March when he left the rue Dauphine for healthier climes. But his friendships with Audoux and Péguy grew very gradually, and the progress of the book was more gradual still – except for one or two dramatic surges of inspiration, like that notable day in September when he announced to one and all that he had found his 'road to Damascus'. So it may be best to establish Fournier, first in his flat and then in his job, before describing the new friends who, in their various ways, were to influence the writing of his book.

On 4 April he wrote from the new flat (2 rue Cassini) to Jacques and Isabelle, who were in Bordeaux for the Easter holidays. 'I tried to write to you yesterday, but in two minutes my head was over-heating, like an engine revving in neutral.' This condition, which he called his neurasthenia, he put down to the first École Normale exam. 'But I think the air here is going to save me: in the morning you feel it's come to you across a stream where poplars grow.' The image could have come straight out of *Pelléas*; yet it originated in that many-windowed fourth floor salon on the corner of rues Cassini and Faubourg Saint-Jacques.

This is a calm, provincial district of hospitals and convents. The Santé Prison and Samuel Beckett's flat are just round the corner. White-coated doctors from Cochin flit past the light, airy edifice which dates from 1900 and so was newish when the Fourniers moved in. Looking up at it today from the street below, one can quite easily see Fournier standing there on the curved corner balcony in April 1910, breathing in deeply the fresher air and accepting joyfully the challenge ahead. At the time, he called that room the 'house of glass' in allusion to Rimbaud's great greenhouse, where the children in mourning examined the marvellous pictures (*Les Illuminations: Aprés le déluge*). 'From time to time I go out on the balcony and let the damp wind lean against my cheek. All alone at the level of the roofs, I'm someone who sees without being seen, and is happy.' He had just lived his first morning in the new home. 'You'll see how it is, the first awakening: it was like my first morning in Paris. . .' (He had conveniently forgotten what his first morning in Paris had really been like.)

He now asked Rouché for regular work on the strength of the couple of short pieces he had already contributed to the *Grande Revue*, suggesting he might handle art notes: not a very important assignment but a beginning. From this moment he became a journalist, even when he was other things too, such as politician's secretary or best-selling novelist. And almost at once – in the May week that Edward VII died – he moved from the *Grande Revue* to a daily newspaper, *Paris-Journal*, where, for two whole years, he held down the job of literary columnist against the best talent in Paris: a remarkable achievement for a man of Fournier's temperament.

The lively *Paris-Journal* (not to be confused with the better known *Le Petit-Journal* or *Le Journal*) had its office in an apartment building (no longer there) on a corner near the Bourse, at 50 rue Notre-Dame-des-Victoires. The literary director was Charles Morice, who was not the old hack he is sometimes dubbed; his perceptive piece on Jules Laforgue in *La Littérature de tout à l'heure*, written as early as 1889, stands to his eternal credit. But perhaps even more significant was Fournier's actual room-mate at the paper, the art critic André Salmon, one of the early champions of Picasso and the new painters.

A smart operator who delivered his three columns a day, Salmon looked across with amusement at his new colleague, who was for ever scoring out adjectives and substituting new ones. But Fournier soon settled down: thanks to his voluminous correspondence with Jacques he had acquired a certain facility and could knock off literary gossip without too much strain. After earning one sou a day as a second-class soldier he was now earning two sous (10 centimes) a line. If he could turn in half a column, or 100 lines, it added up to ten francs a night. A college in Margate had offered him 500 frs a term for a daily stint of 90 minutes teaching French but, after some

Paris-Journal

GÉRAULT-RICHARD, Directeur

nt encore, mais il ne manquera
gtemps, et ce sont les poètes qui
porter. Voici comment.
..sseur de Vanier — premier
.. l'œuvre complète de Ver.
M. Messein, qui s'assure par
iative la sympathie des lettrés,
.. un hommage collectif de nos
.. poètes à la mémoire de Ver-
éditeur prend à sa charge les
la publication, dont les béné-
francs l'exemplaire au mini-
iront intégralement à la sous-
que rouvre, à la même minute,
..re de France.

..ume, qui sera comme le livre
a Poésie contemporaine, s'enri-
que jour d'une page nouvelle.
..ra en septembre et l'on y *doit*
.. dès aujourd'hui.

.. pouvons-nous nous promettre
..rer dans quelques mois, en éri-
.. monument de notre Verlaine,
..en l'un des plus divins chan-
..tous les temps. — Je ne dis pas
..larités de cette fête ne se mêlera

LES QUINZE MILLE

..laires, et qui ressuscitent, figurent deux pro-
..diges : la délicate fougère de l'Arkansas et
la rose biblique de Jéricho. Plus étonnante

LA GRÈVE
DES
Chemins de Fer du Sud

Les transactions interrompues
sur tout le réseau

*Est-ce une manœuvre de la C. G. T.
C'est l'opinion du directeur de la Com
pagnie. - Fils télégraphiques sabotés*

Nice, 30 mai. — *Dépêche particulière
« Paris-Journal ».* — La grève des e
ployés des chemins de fer du Sud de
France continue. Les voies sont toujou
gardées par les gendarmes, qui n'ont d'a
leurs pas à intervenir. La situation s
néanmoins aggravée, puisque la Comp
..nie avait pu, hier assurer le départ et
retour d'un train de Nice à Puget-Tl
niers et Annot (Basses-Alpes) et n'a pu
faire aujourd'hui.

Se référant au vœu de la loi sur l'ar
trage, le juge de paix avait convoqué
membres du comité de grève en son ca
net. Ceux-ci ne se sont pas rendus à
convocation, prétextant qu'ils ne con

quick arithmetic, he still opted for *Paris-Journal* and rightly
so – for it offered certain spin-offs: in a short time he would
come to know everyone in literary Paris; and it did his style
no harm at all to drop the prose-poems for some hack-report-
ing.

Salmon and Fournier were neighbours on the Left Bank, as
well as at the office. The art critic lived in the rue Joseph-Bara,
only a stone's throw from the literary columnist. Often they
returned from work on the top of the same two-horse omnibus
(Palais Royal-Montsouris), alighting at the Café de la Rotonde
together. Salmon was always happy to use his expertise to
extricate his young colleague from such occupational threats
as duels, the Paris equivalent at that time to libel actions. It is
striking to see the amateur doodler of prose-poems become a
professional journalist in what seems the twinkling of an eye.
He was soon reproaching Jacques: 'Have you seen my new
feature called *Women Thinking*? I quote just one sentence from
every new book written by a woman. You miss so much by
not reading my column.'

In fact, Fournier could soon find his way around as well as
Salmon himself. Suspecting that the management were cutting

down on the space allotted him, he got Bichet (who had just won a sensational first place in the *agrégation* exam) to send in a stiff protest as from a leading member of the educational profession: 'Many of us buy your esteemed journal uniquely for its brilliant *Courrier Littéraire*. It would indeed be regrettable if. . .' The ploy worked like a charm, and one is reminded of the adroit *insouciance* with which the gentle Laforgue picked up similar bad habits from his wily publisher Léon Vanier. Two years later, when the job at *Paris-Journal* finally ended, Fournier was always able to pick up useful pocket-money from *L'Intransigeant* and other papers. He had become an accomplished journalist and need never have starved.

Marguerite Audoux

Marguerite Audoux, whom he met in the course of the year, was an orphan from Bourges, who became a shepherdess on an isolated farm in the Sologne. Later she came to Paris, where she worked as a dressmaker until her eyesight failed. Then a *berrichon* friend, Michel Yell, a postal clerk at the Gare de l'Est who wrote in his spare time, introduced her to Charles-Louis Philippe, author of *Bubu de Montparnasse*, a low-life tale of pimps and prostitutes that manages to be immensely moving. She soon became a popular member of his group, attending all the famous lunches at the Crémerie Brunat on the Ile Saint-Louis, and the regular expeditions to Carnetin, a village on the Marne discovered by Yell. None of the group was greatly surprised when Marguerite herself began to write. The painter Francis Jourdain brought her to the attention of the energetic critic Octave Mirbeau, and her first novel was duly serialized in the *Grande Revue* during May and June 1910.

Marie-Claire was the real-life story – told simply and without self-pity – of how the orphan fell in love with the farmer's son, and how the inappropriate idyll had to be snuffed out. Fournier discovered it while looking for his own art notes, and was so impressed he immediately wrote a piece for *Paris-Journal* and another for the *NRF* (1 November 1910), which began:

> The marvel here lies not in the fact that a dressmaker has written a novel. What needs to be emphasized is the perfect simplicity and extraordinary grandeur of the book. The literature of the past thirty years has probably not produced a hymn to the inner life more beautiful than the second part of *Marie-Claire*, which is set among the peasants of the Sologne [. . .] There are no reservations to be made about an art so simple and so powerful.

Indeed, Jean Giraudoux, who had presented *Marie-Claire* to the readers of the *Grande Revue*, was suspected by many of having written the book himself. For Fournier, however, the link with his native district made it doubly moving. He records having read it 'aloud and in tears' to Gustave Tronche, whose wife (a sister of Mme Lhote) had just died.

At length Fournier found that Mme Audoux was living in a perilously high *sixième* at 10 rue Léopold-Robert (on the sunnier corner of that Montparnasse street as it enters

Boulevard Raspail) and lost no time in seeking her out. She was twice his age (forty-seven) and the friendship was that of a talented writer and a young admirer who sought from her lessons in simplicity. He was also happy to be able, with other members of literary Paris, to play some part in winning for her book the Prix Femina of 1910.

Charles-Louis Philippe

It was sad that her mentor Charles-Louis Philippe did not live to see her triumph. The author of *Bubu* had died, aged thirty-five, a year earlier, and it was Marguerite who quoted his last words in the *NRF* of 15 February 1910: 'I'm travelling through a land called fever, making important discoveries which will be precious for me in the future. I've just turned a somersault in space and I can't tell you what I saw there, but the thing is I mustn't forget it.' Last words uncannily like those of Laforgue, who had said: 'I'm not seeing things as I used to. Not thinking the same way either. Wait till you see what I'll write now.'

Fournier in *Paris-Journal* suggested that an Ile Saint-Louis bridge, the Pont Louis-Philippe, should be re-named 'Pont *Charles*-Louis Philippe'. It was a nice thought.

As for Charles Péguy, he might have been put on earth to be Fournier's friend. He was the personification of integrity, a virtue Henri valued above all others. His Catholicism was cast in a different mould to that of Claudel, so that in this case Fournier could be moved without being overwhelmed. He came from the Orléanais, a region bordering Fournier's own Sologne, and from similar peasant stock: Péguy's grandmother, who could not read but inspired a great writer, was in the classic mould of Maman-Barthe herself. Péguy's other inspiration was Joan of Arc. From humble beginnings he won a scholarship to the École Normale Supérieure and became a writer of masterly prose, which he was just now forsaking for poetry.

Péguy ran a bookshop in the heart of the Latin Quarter at 8 place de la Sorbonne. He was also a publisher and edited *Les Cahiers de la Quinzaine*, one of the great periodicals of pre-war Paris. (T.S. Eliot used to count the days to the next issue.) If anyone ever had ink in his blood, it was Péguy, who spoke in the jargon of printers and had an almost mystical love of the printed word. In his case the craft and the calling were easy bedfellows, the shape and feel of a book being almost as important to him as the contents. Indeed, this was symbolic of his approach to life more generally: he was an idealist with his feet on the ground, his religion the more ardent for being earthy.

When Fournier began his 'Courrier Littéraire' for *Paris-Journal* it was natural that one of his first ports of call should be the little *librairie* in the Place de la Sorbonne. Here is how he described its owner:

> Bustling and short-sighted, he has the stubborn look of a peasant shopkeeper. He always seems to be dressed in homespun but this may be due, not so much to the quality of the cloth, as to the ardent and passionate nature of his spirit. In his shop he sells ideas: ideas which set him in a fever, wear him out and finally ruin him. Whenever he discovers a new idea, he becomes a professor in order to explain it. He becomes drunk with his own intelligence and lines up arguments as Rabelais lined up epithets. If need be, to make a point, he will make a joke, like a teacher in the classroom. To illuminate the many different facets of an

idea, he will become poet and visionary. In a note to subscribers he will not hesitate to evoke the heat and dust of the Battle of Wagram. At this very moment it is his mission to show that there have always been mystics in France, today as in Joan of Arc's day. . .

Besides the ink in Péguy's blood, there was also a fair sprinkling of holy water. Fournier found in him what he had already found in Dostoevsky's Prince Myshkin: a form of Christianity to which he could respond, even if it seemed heresy to many. As Geoffrey Hill has said, 'Péguy rediscovered the solitary ardours of faith but not the consolations of religious practice'. His was the kind of religious sense which shares space with an earthy sense of wonder. It was not until the end of the summer holidays that Fournier sent him the declaration which sealed their friendship:

> I was walking with my father in the little village of Nançay (near Salbris in Sologne) where he was born. He showed me the old school building, with its three narrow windows looking on to the street, and said: 'It was a morning like this when the Uhlans arrived. Old Gérault, the *instituteur*, went deathly pale and told us all to go home. Locking up the school, he kept repeating, 'It's them all right, it's them all right.'
> I could see and feel it all. 'It's them all right.' It wasn't just history any more. . . Well, on every page of your books I experience that same emotion. Above all I like the way you write about the Gospels, placing the Apostles' feet so firmly on the ground, and evoking things always in an immediate, living and human way. The Church itself so often makes the Gospels seem sad and dead. Yet looked at and lived through anew, they are the most beautiful and passionate stories in the world.

That particular autumn Péguy and Fournier were drawn together by their interest in Marguerite Audoux and the campaign to support her book. In the years that followed they became woven into the very fabric of each other's lives. Their friendship, in fact, was to last till the end of those lives – a matter of four short years.

Charles Péguy

Cahiers de la Quinzaine, 8, rue de la Sorbonne, rez-de-chaussée, Paris, cinquième arrondissement

mercredi 3 janvier 1912

Fournier appelez-moi Péguy tout court, quand vous

m'écrivez. Je vous assure que je l'ai bien mérité.

Péguy

Péguy to Fournier: 'call me just Péguy when you write. . .'
Fournier to Péguy: ingredients of LGM include 'magic lantern. . . phantas-
magoria. . . Russian Ballet. . . English adventure'

Lundi 7 juillet 1913.

TRIE-LA-VILLE
par **TRIE-CHATEAU**
(OISE)
Teleph. N°3 TRIE-CHATEAU

Mon cher Péguy,

Votre mot ne me surprend pas. Mais il me cause un profond chagrin. Je savais que vous ne voudriez pas aimer le grand Meaulnes. Et pourtant, je vous l'ai dit déjà, le peu de volupté qu'il y a, le peu de lanterne magique, de fantasmagorie, de ballet russe et d'aventure anglaise est racheté par un si long regret, une si étroite peine!

Fournier met Jeanne Bruneau, who was to become the 'Valen-tine' of his novel, in February 1910, and the meeting probably took place on the Quai aux Fleurs near Notre-Dame. Jeanne was a year older than Henri and worked precariously as a freelance *modiste*, making hats at home in a flat which she shared with her elder sister, behind the cathedral at 10 rue Chanoinesse. A handsome house with an attractive iron bal-cony on the topmost floor, the place still stands on the corner of the narrow rue des Chantres. On the wall is a plaque com-memorating a latter-day singer, one Pierre Tremouillet, 'le chansonnier-humoriste', who must have been there at the same time as Jeanne. The rue des Chantres, leading directly to the Quai aux Fleurs, was also a favourite subject of the pioneer photographer Eugène Atget, another contemporary of Jeanne's – but, as he rigorously excluded humans from his atmospheric studies, there is little chance of finding Jeanne lurking in one of his misty backgrounds.

During the period of their liaison (two or three years), Henri lived at home with his parents, visiting Jeanne regularly. She was a *berrichonne* with a slight accent of Bourges which delighted him. Henri's sister Isabelle, who knew the girl and the flat, has explained that she sold hats to a wholesaler and earned only just enough to live on – but even this meagre income dried up at certain times of the year, when she had to rely on some friend or other to help her out. Henri could accept this arrangement if the friend happened to be himself – and one of her rent receipts is in the Fournier papers – but he was appalled that she could allow herself to be bailed out in the same way by other men. He found it impossible to accept the cynicism she had acquired in the course of a difficult life. 'I have a body, a heart and no soul', she used to say. And Fournier would agonize.

But there is something else involved: Fournier was always ready to be influenced by literary sources and it so happened that, in March 1910 , a few days after his first meeting with Jeanne, he read Dostoevsky's *Notes from Underground*. It tells of the tragic Lisa, whom the narrator meets in a brothel and whom he lectures on morality for several pages without once asking himself, 'And you, with your fine morals, what are *you* doing here?' A tortured relationship follows, full of ambiguities, during whch the narrator forces himself to admit

Jeanne Bruneau

his own real feelings. The pitiless examination of so many contradictory motives fill him with panic, so that he cries, 'How I hated her at that moment! But how that hatred drew me towards her! The hatred multiplied the love, and the result was almost like revenge.' All his guilt and shame are taken out sadistically on the girl, whose only reaction is bewilderment, and a belief that the man confronting her is ill. There emerges from the story, as so often with Dostoevsky, the feeling that women are more attuned to real life than men, and this was clearly so in the case of Jeanne-Henri. Like the narrator, Henri was presented at this time with a host of new complications which overwhelmed him – but, as a writer, he must have understood that man's secret desires, however absurd or even repellent, are what make him human. Fournier had stumbled on a rich new vein of realism, which he was never able fully to exploit but which forced him to re-examine some of his old literary credos. It is a striking fact that the photograph of Jeanne Bruneau, reproduced here for the first time and presumably taken by Henri, could serve quite adequately as a portrait of Dostoevsky's Lisa.

On the other hand, his letters are full of delicate reminders which leave no doubt of his tender feelings towards the girl:

I remember the first time we met: your way of suddenly looking at me, as one looks at someone who isn't telling the truth [. . .] and the way you kissed my forehead and said, 'That's the way you should be kissed, you're just a little boy' [. . .] and how on Tuesday, when we were walking behind your sister in the rue Béranger, I laughed at something childish you said, and you quickly squeezed my arm.

There was a great deal he could share with Jeanne and probably – as Seurel says of Meaulnes and Valentine (*LGM*, p. 263) – she might have made him an excellent wife. 'I'm working like mad,' he says on 6 September 1910, 'including several hours a day on the book!'

Today I hope to finish the chapter on our trip to Orgeville and I've begun a story for *Paris-Journal*, which is getting to be as revolting as all the other rags. I'm also doing a note on *Marie-Claire* for the *NRF*. I feel terribly ambitious: I've just been paid 10 frs a page for a piece in the *Grande Revue*. Remember when we needed that sort of money so badly? But we got through in the end, didn't we? Money problems always come right in the end, it's the other sort that don't. Today is a typical September morning, misty and sentimental. A damp bee has just come into the room, and he is sitting on the gilt clasp of our Agenda.

Orgeville was a kind of artists' colony, near Evreux, in Normandy, where André and Marguerite Lhote were staying. It was there, about the same time, that Raoul Dufy made his famous woodcuts for Apollinaire's *Bestiaire*. During the visit – in a well-meant gesture that went wrong – Jeanne handed over a packet of love-letters from a former lover who had killed himself. Her offer that Henri could destroy them only exacerbated his jealousy and led to one of their most painful rows, during which he actually threw great chunks of earth at her.

Soon after this we find Fournier telling his sister that he has broken with Jeanne for ever:

There was something appealingly childlike about her. I don't think it was a great love, more of a violent attachment [. . .] I've already left her five or six times before, because of something she said or some memory she dredged up. Then she'd

ask me to return, and I did [. . .] But this time she told me,
'All right, I'll go back to my other friend, I never really
loved you anyway'.

He was glad (he told his sister). The relief was tremendous.
'I feel young again. It's a secret joy, like being re-born.' To
Bichet he went farther still. '*Quelle victoire!*' he proclaimed.
It did not sound like a victory when he returned to the
subject in a letter to Jacques the following week:

> When I dreamt of her last night, she was wearing one of
> her dresses that I'd forgotten: with her little starched white
> collar she looked like a guilty pierrot [. . .] I saw her from
> the train, but the train didn't stop. The three chapters in
> my book that I've finished are all devoted to her, but the
> hidden emotion in those chapters comes from another pre-
> sence.

He is referring, of course, to 'Yvonne de Galais', the ideal
woman, for whom 'Valentine', the all too human one, is no
match. He suggests that a suitable epigraph for *Le Grand
Meaulnes* might well be the words of Shelley: 'Some of us
have, in a prior existence, been in love with Antigone, and
that makes us find no full content in any mortal tie.' The difference, he explains to Jacques, is that he met his own Antigone
(Mlle de Quiévrecourt) in this life, not in a prior one.

> And here's the real reason why I left Jeanne: I'm not
> interested in just having a mistress, I want love. Love in the
> sense of vertigo. Love as a sacrifice and the last word on
> everything. The thing alongside which nothing else exists.
> Love as the grand departure after setting ablaze the four
> corners of the land.

On 19 October he wrote to Jacques again: a letter delivered
by hand to the couple's new flat on the third floor of 15 rue
Froidevaux, at the south-east corner of Montparnasse cemetery. Henri, who was still living with his parents in rue Cassini,
reported that the other evening he had found Jeanne sitting on
a bench in the Avenue de l'Observatoire. He had felt sorry
for her, returned to her, but then left her again. Yet, two
months later, while she was recovering from an illness at
Bourges, he wrote to her every day.

A cutting from a popular English weekly, sent by Fournier to Jeanne, 'because the girl has your hairstyle'

5 December – I was sad when I left you. I didn't know where to go or what to do. Outside a shop in the rue Bonaparte I was looking at some German engravings when someone touched my arm, saying, 'Good morning, elegant young man.' It was Jacques Copeau, who was wandering around just like me. [Then a member of the *NRF* team, Copeau was later to run the famous Vieux-Colombier experimental theatre.] So we spent the morning at the Louvre together and, when we came out, it started to rain and we talked all the more furiously. He told me about his friendship with Gide. I couldn't decide to leave him, I was so pleased to have found a friend. It was night already when I left for the paper.

6 December – Don't you think you were wrong not to stick to the diet they prescribed, even for just a while? Now, if you'd been a good girl I'd have told you many things: for instance, how I went to see Marguerite Audoux for five minutes and stayed for two hours. She said I reminded her of the young men of her youth; I told her that you saw me as a peasant too – but a mad, bad one.

7 December – Tonight I'm going to a concert with the others. They're doing Musorgsky's song-cycle 'The Nursery' ('La chambre d'enfants') and there was a ticket for you. I like the idea of giving you these small pleasures, but tonight my head is heavy and empty because the concert is just going to tire me and I'd rather be in the country with you.

9 December – Last night I dreamt I was in the field opposite my parents' house [at Epineuil]. It was night and I hardly recognized it. A wonderful night it was, with every now and then flashes of blue lightning and people's voices calling out to one another. But I stayed there in the field, frightened and ill. I shouted, but no one in the sleeping house replied.

11 December – I desired you very much, my darling, all through this Sunday. There was a time, on Sundays in the country, when the evenings were a long, silent paradise. In those days little girls wore fur hats and, when they looked at picture books, sitting on the thick carpet, they pressed their hot cheeks against mine.

On 16 February he told Bichet that he had once again left Jeanne. 'I'm striding through the town like a young god,' he said. 'But for how long?'

Jeanne could hardly have been surprised by her subsequent appearance as Valentine in *Le Grand Meaulnes* – Henri had given her fair warning of his intentions.[1] Valentine first appears in Jeanne's little black dress, with the collar that makes her look like a guilty pierrot. We learn that she comes from Bourges, that she lives with her sister near Notre-Dame and works as a dressmaker. The real-life visit of Henri and Jeanne to the Lhotes in Normandy, as well as an unchronicled visit by Henri to Jeanne's mother at Bourges, both become scenes in the novel. Jeanne would certainly have recognized Frantz's would-be suicide as having been suggested by her own lover's actual suicide. When it comes to the reasons for the split between Valentine and Frantz, these are given in such detail that they actually help us to understand the estrangements of

[1] For references to Valentine in *LGM* see pp. 69-70, 72-4, 88-9, 91, 160-1, 187-90, 254-73.

Jeanne and Henri. It is a case of characters in fiction revealing the secrets of their real-life counterparts. And so we learn that when Jeanne went back to her lover, it was because she felt unworthy of Henri and was happier making her sacrifice than being his wife. She had never experienced any real hope of happiness with him because he saw only an imaginary Jeanne. He could not accept that she was full of faults, that she was a dressmaker and not a princess. They would have been very unhappy. And besides, he was too young for her.

In almost every letter now, news about Jeanne is juxtaposed with news about the book. During a break at La Chapelle he reports:

> For a fortnight I pressed on with the book in a highly artificial way, as I'd begun. Nothing much came of this. In the end I dropped that approach, and one evening found my 'road to Damascus'. I began to write simply, directly, as I would in a letter, with short paragraphs, smooth and voluptuous, telling a simple story as if it were my own. I threw overboard all my entangling abstractions and philosophy. And what's marvellous is that the essence of the thing remains: it's still my book.

And a week later:

> All those old, half-known, half-forgotten things. . . I was mad to think they'd be enough. It was the folly of Symbolism. From now on, those things will occupy, in my book, exactly the place they occupy in life: that faint stirring of emotion that comes to me at the bend of a road, or end of a paragraph.

As Jacques said later, Symbolism had dispensed with so many elements of life judged to be crude and vulgar that, in the end, the readers dispensed with Symbolism itself:

> There appeared a blinding light, which lit up our path. Fournier saw it first and was the first to act. We had to break with Symbolism and the whole mental arsenal it proposed. We had to shake ourselves free from the mind and the heart, and seize upon objects and facts, placing them carefully between the reader and the emotion we wished him to experience [. . .] Fournier found his real aptitudes and strength when he realized he was a novelist. In one bound

he released himself from dream, and grasped real life with all its accidents. Henceforth he would count solely on things he had scrupulously observed to reveal the emotion that comes 'at the bend of a road or the end of a paragraph.'

From now on Fournier could only believe in the marvellous when it sprang from real life. It was now he decided he would begin his book in the most humdrum way possible, and then gently take the reader by the hand and lead him into the fantastic. He had found the secret which makes the first part of *Le Grand Meaulnes* so effective.

At the end of 1910 he wrote a slight piece called 'Le Miracle de la fermière', possibly the first glimmer of his new manner. Péguy was perceptive enough to notice this and to say, 'When you have seven like this, bring them to me and I'll publish them. But remember, there must be seven: it's a sacred number.' And later, when another short piece 'Portrait' was published in the *NRF*, Péguy's comment was, 'You'll go far, Fournier, and don't forget it was I who told you so.'

The likely original of the lost domain: Château de Loroy (also opposite page)

A silent witness to Fournier's life in Paris during the period October 1910 to September 1911 was the poet T. S. Eliot, who went to him for French lessons. At the time, as we have seen, he was an impecunious journalist paid by the line. He needed to find ways of bolstering his income and one of them was to teach. At first he offered André Gide English lessons for five francs an hour, but Gide plumped for the Berlitz School instead. In the summer of 1910 Fournier had just one pupil, a certain Dubois whom he instructed in philosophy, but Dubois was a bad payer. There is a letter recording Fournier's regret that he cannot help Jeanne at a critical moment because of Dubois's recalcitrance. The arrival that autumn from America of Mr T. S. Eliot could not have been better timed.

Eliot booked a room at 9 rue de l'Université, just round the corner from the church of Saint-Germain-des-Prés. The place was not a *pension de famille*, as sometimes described, but a *maison meublée* run by a Mme Mahieu. Probably recommended to him by Ezra Pound, it was soon to become the Hôtel Lenox, which is what it remains today.

From the Lenox of 1910-11 Eliot would sally forth in the small hours to savour the Paris night and all its terrors, which he could not have done if the place had been a genteel *pension*. In his series of short unpublished poems of the time, examined by Lyndall Gordon *(Eliot's early years)* in the New York Public Library, there is much talk of garrets. One poem is called precisely 'Agony in a garret'. In others 'a poet in a gloomy garret gazes at the constellations and they do not enlighten him. . . the stir of habit takes the poet back to his garret at four in the morning.' Lyndall Gordon sums it all up as 'the seedy life of the would-be artist up six dingy flights of stairs', a phrase that describes exactly the ubiquitous *sixième* or top-floor room known to generations of Paris students. And not only students: one thinks of Baudelaire in his own top room at the Hôtel de Dieppe, 22 rue d'Amsterdam, in the dark years after 1859. No doubt Eliot's was a different sort of desperation, and of shorter duration, but he too conjured great work from the experience of Paris: 'Rhapsody on a windy night' can worthily stand beside 'Les Sept Vieillards'.

The arrangement between Fournier and TSE, one guesses, quickly developed. Fournier's English had benefited from the spell in Chiswick: it was a fair match for Eliot's French, they could communicate with ease. Why is it, then, that almost nothing is known of the relationship. Fournier's English biographer, Robert Gibson, tackled Eliot on the question in 1951, but the interview rated only a paragraph in *The Land without a name*. Much as one would have liked to think that Eliot and Fournier spent happy hours discussing the writers who meant most to them, there is no evidence that they did anything of the kind. Apparently the talk was all of Gide and Claudel. We learn, for instance, that Fournier communicated to Eliot his enthusiasm for Gide's *Paludes*. No mention of Laforgue, who inspired that story. Eliot was a keen reader of *Les Cahiers de la Quinzaine*, whose editor was by now Fournier's close friend Charles Péguy. No mention of Péguy. Charles-Louis Philippe's *Bubu de Montparnasse* was considered by Eliot to be a symbol of the Paris of 1910, standing for Paris as some of Dicken's novels stand for London. But no mention of Philippe.

Apart from polishing his pupil's French, Fournier seems to have performed two major services for Eliot. He persuaded him to read Victor Derély's French translation of *Crime and Punishment* (the one that Laforge himself had read in 1885), thus leaving an indelible mark on 'Prufrock'. Then, when Eliot needed advice on some projected Sorbonne thesis, Fournier took him along to meet his brother-in-law Jacques Rivière. The ultimate effect of that was to bring together the *NRF* and *The Criterion* as the spearhead of Anglo-French literary collaboration.

And, apart from his regular payments, what did Eliot do for Fournier? No doubt he supplied valuable material for the *Paris-Journal* column. . . they must also have exchanged views on English literature in general. . . one can only hope that a few more details one day will emerge.[1]

Despite their financial and other problems, Henri and Jeanne were still able to participate in the social life of Paris at one of its most brilliant periods. First and foremost there was the ballet. After their Paris début the previous year at the Châtelet, the Ballets Russes were, in the summer of 1910, consolidating their reputation in a new season at the Opera. Henri writes to Lhote on 3 July:

> We went with Jacques to the Russian Ballet, and I must say he irritated me a little: how can a stage performance, a manifestation of art, loom *to that extent* in a person's life? For Jacques today is as mad about Nijinsky and Ida Rubinstein and the lady in the box office at the Russian Ballet, as he once was about Mary Garden and Jean Périer and the man in the music-shop who sold the score of *Pelléas*! The other night, during *Prince Igor*, he clung to me, shaken and breathless! You know how I love Jacques but that sort of thing quite worries me – probably because of my austere and 'serious' upbringing, when art played second fiddle to life, and we even had to hide ourselves to read the prize-books. Where I blame him is that for a mere performance he'll neglect the marvels of life. On our way to the theatre, for instance, I was so struck by the sight of a blacksmith and his girl holding hands in the street that I'd gladly have missed part of the ballet to stay and watch. That said, though, the Opera ballets are unique and perfect. *Prince Igor* is the savage ultimate in earthly dance, while Isadora Duncan evokes a paradise morning in all its purity. *Carnaval* is the joyous Italian carnival imagined anew by barbarians. It reminded me of the old days when, between the curtains of a booth on the village square, there appeared the pure white face of a gangling pierrot: with pathetic, stifled cries, he'd fill a rag doll with porridge and fling it at the audience.[2]

[1] See Appendix.
[2] *Cahiers du Musée National d'Art Moderne*, No. 4, 253.

Clearly the fantasy side of *Le Grand Meaulnes* owed much to Russian Ballet. Ganache in the book is that same gangling Italian pierrot, and even the two girls in Directoire hats – who might have been inspired by the girls of Chiswick in 1905 – could equally have been the girls of *Carnaval*: 'those fair creatures in crinolines', as Jean Cocteau described them, 'their braids and ringlets peeping out from under coal-scuttles and camellias'. In fact, the seven chapters of the book which take place in the mysterious domain can almost be seen as the libretto for a one-act romantic ballet (music by Schumann, decor and costumes by Bakst, choreography by Fokine), skilfully inserted into an otherwise realistic novel by Alain-Fournier. The ballet begins as Meaulnes approaches along the forest path and hears the sound of children's voices (*LGM*, p. 58); it ends when the old coach lurches off, leaving him by the roadside in the bleak morning light (*LGM*, p. 97).

Despite Rivière's rapture at the ballet, it was actually Fournier who showed a more genuine appreciation. He gently castigates his friend after a performance of *Petrushka* the following year:

> I don't see it at all like you. For me it is neither boisterous, light nor bouncing; I'd call it disturbing, brooding and complex – as baffling and precise as a dream. Imagine the streets of an unknown town through which you rush by night, until you reach the tenth open square and find it is the same as the first one, with the same fair going on and the same drum being beaten. And after you reach your thirtieth room you begin to feel a slight anxiety and wonder if you'll ever get out. But then three puppets burst through the wallpaper and you're back at the fairground, ready to learn the truth at last of Petrushka, his tragic story and clockwork loves. It's a prodigious invention, both amusing and tragic, logical and ludicrous, only to be compared to the structure of a recurring dream, which is always the same and always different – the dream in which I gallop, roaring with laughter, through all the rooms of my mind. Yet from your description one might think *Petrushka* was another *Prince Igor*, a ballet that expressed the sheer joy of dance and nothing more. For me it is a work of fantasy and imagination, comparable to the comedies of Shakespeare.

Under the influence of the Russians, Fournier was moving towards a tougher form of art, rich in texture: Dostoevsky leavened by Diaghilev. His growing interest in Dostoevsky augured well for his future as a writer. When he mentioned Dostoevsky, he was perceptive, as in this note on *The Adolescent*:

From that wildly confused beginning I felt the fever mount within me. At the end of the first part I was already overwhelmed. And here's a detail: the extraordinary grandeur that Dostoevsky can give to something like the seedy sex ads in a newspaper. It tells you that at some time he himself was obsessed by them, impelled by some tawdry desire but hesitating as always between good and evil, struggling endlessly against either the one or the other. Setting out from evil surroundings to do evil, and then acting like a great heroic saint. In a complete portrait of the man you would have to show him like that: his head on fire, his hands all sweaty, foraging in the fourth page of some filthy rag, and not knowing if it will all end in his raping an unknown woman, or handing over to her everything he has in the world.

In the last months of his life Fournier busied himself with two plans: a novel called *Colombe Blanchet* and a play called *La Maison dans la forêt*. Both were unfinished and probably would always have remained so: he was outgrowing such timid themes. As source material for the novel he *might* have written, there were more possibilities in the drunken Captain Matharan, whom he met during his twenty-eight day period of reserve training at Mirande in September 1911. In a letter to Jacques he described waiting to go on night-ops and listening to the captain as he roamed about in the next room, knocking over the furniture and shouting: 'They'd like to lock me up, the bastards.' Though only thirty-eight he had become an alcoholic after the death of his wife and his hair was completely white. Fournier watched him in the moonlight that slanted through an open window: despite his incredible violence, Fournier liked the man. He even liked that pointed, badger face, so red that it was almost black – but most of all he liked the way the Captain spoke of his past life and people he had known.

Later that night Captain Matharan sought Fournier out and apologized to him for something completely inconsequential; and next morning, during discussion about manoevres, he made further baffling remarks that nobody understood. Five minutes later, on the parade ground, he had a fit and fell off his horse. 'I shall never forget that brutal face covered in blood, the trembling lips, the whites of the eyes, and the hands clenched as if to ward off an invading presence.' But next day, with hideously swollen countenance, he was back on his horse and Fournier later heard that he'd fathered a son, married the mother, and was drinking less.

Immediately after the spell at Mirande, Fournier went to stay with Gide in Normandy, having been persuaded to do so by Jacques' ecstatic report of a similar visit when he and Isabelle had found 'an enchanted house. . . a paradise. . . and the Gides delicious'. Fournier, too, found life at Cuverville delicious: appropriately enough, this was the moment when his short piece 'Portrait' appeared in the *NRF*, a small landmark in his career.

He was also developing a taste for painting. Up till now it had always been Jacques who made the running in art appreciation; now Henri sought out new painters and awarded them marks for originality. Two of his new favourites were Braque and Van Dongen, while his liking for lesser figures was also interesting. After spending varnishing day at the Salon des Independants of 1911 he writes: 'I adore [le Douanier] Rousseau. If it weren't too late, I'd buy a landscape. There's so much grace and faith there, I'm sure Apollinaire's right to call the man an angel.'

Towards the end of 1911, Jacques and Isabelle had their first child, a daughter Jacqueline. Precisely at this moment, despite his extra responsibilities, Jacques was forced to give up his teaching job at the Collège Stanislas in Montparnasse because he could not keep order in class. The merciless rioting of French schoolboys has driven saner men than Jacques to distraction. Henri Fournier himself had often raised the roof at Lakanal, and could well understand his brother-in-law's predicament. One fine day Jacques just walked out of his class, out of the school and out of teaching forever. André Gide came to the rescue with a dramatic coup, appointing Jacques

Isabelle Rivière with Jacqueline, 1911

Rivière editor of the *Nouvelle Revue Française*.

As for Henri, he finished the year with an adventure, possibly his most light-hearted love-affair. Describing it to Lhote he said he was going out with a girl he wasn't in love with, but whom he liked because she was so slim and amusing: she was so funny that sometimes people turned round in the street to laugh. As Isabelle described it (*Images*, p. 321):

He was returning from the theatre about midnight when he passed a group of revellers in opera hats and cloaks. To his amazement a girl suddenly detached herself from the group and joined him without a word, walking home quietly at his side as if she had known him all her life.

This was Henriette, a young music-hall singer. Their liaison ended with a jolt a few weeks later when the poste restante

people gave him a letter she had meant for someone else. His
farewell note to the singer is a classic of its kind:

> What are we doing together, you and I? You, with your
> little body, straight as a whistle from top to toe, made for
> dancing and warbling and having fun! What is the point of
> our liaison? If I'd been honest I'd have ended it long ago.
> We were travelling in opposite directions and held out hands
> [. . .] but now it's time to move on again. I'd like our love
> to have been a tale of two children who cut school and stole
> nuts together: a game we played, but now it's over and no
> regrets. I like you very much but the trouble is that your
> happiness isn't mine – we're not looking for the same
> paradise.

8 · *High Society (1912-1913)*

On 10 April 1912 Fournier contributed his last paragraph of literary gossip to the ailing *Paris-Journal* and found himself out of a job. He could always have gone on with *L'Intransigeant*, but he had reached the point in *Le Grand Meaulnes* when he wished desperately to finish the book. He therefore set out to find less arduous work than the time-consuming diary assignment.

Charles Péguy knew what Fournier wanted, and found it for him. A friend of his in the Army Reserve was a young officer, Claude Casimir-Perier, son of the late President of the Republic. As a means of making his way into politics, Casimir-Perier planned to produce a massive tome called *Brest: port transatlantique*, on which Fournier's journalistic skills could be useful. Claude's wife, the actress Simone, was just then returning from an American tour, so Péguy (whom she adored) formed the plan of waylaying her as she stepped on to French soil – all in the good cause of getting his friend a job. The plan was slightly complicated by her landing first in England, to complete some unfinished business, so the port of her homecoming turned out to be Dieppe. But when the boat arrived, Péguy was there, at the end of the mole, holding her pet dog and wearing a yachting cap bought specially for the occasion chez Delion. While driving to Simone's country house at Trie-la-ville, near Gisors, he sang to her the praises of a certain Alain-Fournier, with the result that the actress was not unprepared when Henri turned up at her apartment in Paris the following day.

Simone had been born Pauline Benda, the daughter of a rich Jewish banker. Maurice Sachs found her no conventional beauty, 'but the total effect was bewitching'. Brought up in the elegant Faubourg Saint-Honoré, she had gone to school

Simone: à la scene

. . . en ville

at the local Lycée Racine, and later came to the notice of Charles Le Bargy, a star of the Comédie-Française – who proceeded, as she always maintained, to marry her for her money. But at least Le Bargy gave her the chance to try her luck at acting: a chance that she took with both hands and instant success, first under the name of Pauline Prima and later just Simone. She was now a famous actress but, having divorced her first husband (Le Bargy) she was not finding life any easier with her second, whose many interests included other women. She consoled herself with her stage success and her many professional friends, who included playwrights like Henry Bernstein busily engaged on writing vehicles for her spectacular talents.

Charles Le Bargy

She was indeed regarded as Bernstein's born interpreter, her rise to fame having exactly coincided with his own. She had played leads in *Le Détour*, *Le Bercail*, *La Rafale*, *Le Voleur* and *Samson*, usually at the Théâtre du Gymnase on the Grands Boulevards. Since all these were direct, vigorous, almost brutal dramas, full of cut-and-thrust dialogue, Simone had acquired the reputation of herself being a restless, energetic and wilful woman, with a cutting edge to her tongue and violence in every movement. She was supposed to be a lady brimming over with intelligence, but with little use for the soft, smiling, feminine graces. To prove that this was not necessarily so, an account had appeared in the *New York Times* of 21 September 1911 showing that when she set her mind to it, she could charm the hind legs off a donkey, American or otherwise:

Mme Simone Casimir-Perier, the French actress and wife of the son of the late President of France, arrived in New York on the Oceanic yesterday morning to begin her first American tour under the direction of Liebler & Co. She was accompanied by her husband, a maid, a 12-year-old poodle, and numerous trunks, and she went to the Hotel Plaza. In her apartment she held a levee of reporters, managers and friends, and proved to be a most capable hostess. She proved also to be a charming woman, without affectation of any sort, full of earnestness about her work, and with a sort of well-bred good-fellowship.

Mme Casimir-Perier – or Mme Simone, as she is known – is about 30 years old and has been on the stage for nine years. She began acting because she wanted something to do, and because Bernhardt thought it was the best thing for her to attempt. She was born in Paris, and learnt to speak English there in a manner that would put to shame most American or English-born women. Her voice yesterday afternoon had no trace of French accent. Simply dressed in a white gown over a cream-coloured slip, with green shoes and a thin green coat, Mme Simone has a perfect complexion and was quite without make-up. She is an emotional actress and likes plays in which character is developed. 'I am a gay person,' she said,' 'so that when I laugh all the afternoon I do not mind having to cry at night.'

But during the same year, the *New York Times* had published an item of a rather different kind:

Simone

Henry Bernstein
by Cappiello (© DACS 1986)

The widow of M. Casimir-Perier, President of the French Republic, has applied for the appointment of trustees for the fortune of her son, the husband of Mme Simone, divorced wife of M. Le Bargy, of the Comédie-Française. Young Casimir-Perier's mother alleges that he has been guilty of acts of great prodigality and has wasted nearly a quarter of a million dollars.

Simone's Paris apartment where she first met Henri, still stands at 54 avenue de New York (then quai Debilly) on an elegant corner next to the Palais de Chaillot (then Trocadéro). It faces the Eiffel Tower across a great bend of the Seine, but is perhaps a little less prestigious today because of the relentless two-way traffic under its windows along the *quai*. At the dinner-party welcoming her home, she and Fournier at once became friends: so much so that in the weeks that followed she began to monopolize more and more of his time, sometimes

to the detriment of *Brest: Atlantic port*. As an ex-columnist
with many contacts in journalism, it was clear that Fournier
could fill the bill brilliantly as her personal representative.
Before long she was even taking him home for weekends at
Trie, where she and Claude entertained a regular group of
well-wishers headed by Jean Cocteau.

Cocteau greatly admired the voice of Simone and the way
she used it, making it sometimes as quick and precise as a
machine, at other times slow and grave like a viola. And she
was such a keen observer (he said) that people used to think
she was exaggerating when she was telling no more than the
simple truth. A good listener too, she constantly encouraged
her guests (meaning him) with little cries of 'No, it's not possible. . . I don't believe it. . . Do go on.' 'And how we laughed
at Trie, the Casimir-Periers' country house! I remember one
occasion when our laughter became so absolutely crazy that
our sides began to ache and we got cramp and had to sit on
the stairs to recover.' Then, when the windows paled and
twilight brought a little calm, Péguy began to recite Victor
Hugo and after a little while was succeeded by Simone. With
lowered eyes and hands clasped round her knees, she launched
into one of those immense poems that undergraduates know
by heart, all about the mortality of man and how even the
great must die. Cocteau recalled this in later life and imagined
himself back at Trie: 'It's very hot, the grass is buzzing with
bees and the little stream flows on. I'm lying on my stomach
by the cool water and what do I see? Claude Casimir-Perier,
Alain-Fournier, Péguy, all now dead. . .' But we anticipate:
for this was not to happen for another three years. . .

Meanwhile Fournier still wrote the odd piece for *L'Intransigeant*, including a portrait of the poet Léon-Paul Fargue,
whom he interviewed at a rehearsal of the Russian Ballet's
Daphnis and Chloe on 6 June 1912, two days before its historic
première at the Châtelet with Nijinsky and Karsavina. Just a
week later Fournier was carrying out a very different assignment. In thanksgiving for his children's recovery from illness,
Péguy had vowed to walk in pilgrimage to Chartres and back.
Fournier (perhaps partly in gratitude for his new job) agreed
to join him on the first lap, which led from Péguy's little house
at Lozère, south of Paris, to the half-way town of Dourdan.

Jean Cocteau

The walk is commemorated in Péguy's *Présentation de la Beauce à Notre-Dame de Chartres*, a poem of eighty-nine stanzas, each comprising four alexandrines (rhyming a-b-b-a) in which the waving wheat-fields of the Beauce are compared to the swell and heave of the ocean. Even his handwriting looked like tall ears of waving corn – Simone said it resembled that of Louis XIV.

Soon after setting out, the two walkers pass Gometz-le-Châtel ('which has no castle') and Gometz-la-ville ('which isn't a town') proclaiming: 'We come to you from distant Paris,/ having shut up shop for three whole days,/ giving the slip to the old Sorbonne,/ its ancient ways and poor little students.' After descending the hill at Limours, says Péguy: 'We met three or four gendarmes,/ who eyed us somewhat suspiciously / as we scanned the names on the signposts.' The intrepid walkers were obviously looking for the turning to Dourdan, where eventually Péguy spent the night (before plodding on next day to Chartres) while Fournier caught the next train back to Paris. Péguy later published the poem as part of *La*

Tapisserie de Notre-Dame in the *Cahiers de la Quinzaine* for Whitsun 1913 – but Fournier heard it before then and was greatly moved.

It was not only on the road to Chartres that Péguy and Fournier walked together. Jacques Rivière has pictured them deep in conversation on a Paris street:

> They walk together on the Boulevard Saint-Germain, and all the gods of France are with them, conjured up and charmed by their conversation. Joan of Arc is born again, a friendly and protective presence walking between them. All the great ones are there – Joinville, and Saint-Louis too – an assembly both fraternal and divine.

Fournier's first flight

Another enthusiasm of Fournier's is glimpsed on 28 June when he flies for the first time in an aeroplane. 'Just like Peter Pan,' he told his old idol Francis Jammes, the poet. From then on he did not cease to scan the Paris sky: aviation had supplanted motor-racing as his ruling passion.

At the end of July, when Simone and Claude left for their summer home, the Villa Souberbielle at Cambo, in the Pyrenees, Fournier at last had time for other things. While he was walking home one day, along the rue Cassini, a piece of screwed up paper dropped at his feet. It came from a window which, as he looked up, gently closed. On the parachuted message he found an address and an invitation: such was his introduction to Loulette, a blonde neighbour he had not suspected, whose busy husband left her alone all day without any company but her infant son. From then on Fournier used to bundle the two of them into a taxi and take them to the Bois de Boulogne. He enjoyed the atmosphere of domestic bliss thus engendered, and even took his sister along on the outings. Loulette was a tiny doll-like creature, who wore a flower behind her ear and ate sweets all day. Her baby was reportedly almost as big as herself. When Isabelle warned Henri of the danger if he went too far with a married woman, he replied, 'You're absolutely right but it's too late – it happened the first day.' Besides (said Fournier) 'she's so childish it's like playing with a kitten. And so innocent, I think the baby knows more about life than she does.' None the less, they went on seeing each other for almost a year, even after the husband had become convinced that his wife had a lover. 'He threatened to shoot the man if he discovered who it was,' says Isabelle. 'After that their meetings became less frequent, and Henri made a point of leaving his own revolver at home, in case he felt tempted to use it in self-defence.' The fact that Henri habitually carried a gun at this time is not the least surprising thing about the episode.

At the rentrée Simone left on another American tour, from which she sent back a present for Henri. 'Simone has sent me a magnificent volume of Keats,' he told Jacques. 'It contains two portraits, and the smaller one is supposed to look like me.' Simone was right. When we finally traced the edition (Houghton Mifflin, 1899) Alain Rivière readily agreed that the resemblance to his uncle was uncanny. The original is now in the National Portrait Gallery, London.

All this time Fournier was still getting agency reports about the former Yvonne de Quiévrecourt, one of which revealed her current address – ironically it was in the 'transatlantic' port

John Keats by Joseph Severn

Simone in The Paper-chase, *during her*
US tour, winter 1912-13

of Brest. So he sat down and wrote her a long letter, but did not post it. To little Bichet, then working in Budapest, he boasted of what he had done: 'The letter in question resides at this moment in the right-hand pocket of my jacket, and it will be delivered before the end of the year.' In his usual way he passed on some gratuitous advice to Bichet: 'Everything is possible, young man. If something's necessary, it's possible. We suffer from our weaknesses: we die because we do not dare.' This had been the motto of Jacques Coeur, of Bourges, and was therefore not very original. Three weeks later he wrote again to Bichet, but this time more interestingly: he promised to present to his friend , on his return to France at the end of the year, a typed copy of *Le Grand Meaulnes* on a silver platter.

Alas, that charming ceremony never took place. On 27 November, Fournier told Gustave Tronche: 'The good little guy will be here in a month.' And on 20 December Bichet was indeed in Paris, attending an old boys' reunion of the École Normale. After the banquet he was persuaded to try a new experience: a morphine jab. Was he thinking, when he received the overdose from inexpert hands in a sordid hotel room, of Fournier's cry: 'One must dare'? In any case the single shot was fatal and, when Péguy heard of Henri's subsequent distress, he added these lines to his *Présentation de la Beauce à Notre-Dame de Chartres'*: 'We come to pray to you for that poor boy,/ who died like a fool the other day./ Almost on the same day and hour/ as your son was born in the straw./ O Mary, he was not the worst of us./ His faults were few and far between,/ but relentless death which pursues us all/ passed through the tiny hole he made in his skin.'

Fournier wept. He was hearing the poem for the first time in his room at rue Cassini – from Péguy's own lips – and had enjoyed the earlier part with its jocular account of the two pilgrims setting out on their walk. Unprepared for the additional lines, he was greatly moved. That evening (3 January 1913) he wrote to Jacques: 'With the full recognition of what I am saying, I do not think there has been, since Dostoevsky, a man so clearly a man of God as Péguy.'

The Paris papers were less concerned. They gave the news of Bichet's death in five or six lines with the heading:

DEAD PROFESSOR WAS DOPE ADDICT
(MORT D'UN JEUNE PROFESSEUR MORPHINOMANE)

Simone returned from America on 28 January and almost at once began rehearsals for a new play, *Le Secret*, written for her by Henry Bernstein, and in which she would play opposite the rising young star Victor Boucher. But in an interval of learning her lines, she read another new work: *Le Grand Meaulnes* by Alain-Fournier. This happened at Trie on 10-11 February 1913: she stayed up with the book all night and, as dawn was breaking, slipped a note under her secretary's door, expressing her deep admiration.

A couple of days before the *répétition générale* of *Le Secret*, at the *Bouffes-Parisiens* on 20 March, Fournier received sad news from Nançay: his favourite cousin Marie-Rose had died in childbirth. During the hectic theatre preparations he was obliged to keep it to himself since – as Simone's PR – he had to deal with the press and be constantly on call. Eventually *Le Secret* was adjudged the success of the season and as for Simone herself, she 'had the lively charm of a young boy', according to the stage daily *Comoedia*. It was the kind of praise which must have been music to her ears, since she was in fact nine years older than her young companion, with whom she was rapidly falling in love. She had at first thought him impossibly young for her, but then thought again, encouraged in this to some extent by Mme Fournier herself, who never hid her admiration for the famous actress who had befriended her son.

Isabelle and Jacques, on the other hand, remained very much on the defensive, and viewed with irony Simone's efforts to ingratiate herself with the family. After meeting Simone at the Salon des Indépendants Jacques told Isabelle: 'She was charming and already loves me with a pure and faithful love. She thinks the Cubists, too, are charming.' And two days later; 'Your parents are in a box at *Le Secret* this afternoon. Henri is also there – in Simone's dressing-room.'

Henri was conscious of their reserve, and it was to his mother that he was most forthcoming on the subject of his actress friend:

With regard to my book her devotion is truly amazing. She resembles, in this respect, her role in *Le Secret*: she wants the people she loves to be happy through her, and through her alone [. . .] There's a plan being hatched by the publisher Emile-Paul, Simone, Péguy and Simone's cousin to get me the Prix Goncourt, but a condition is that Emile-Paul would publish the book.

This, of course, was dynamite as far as Jacques was concerned, since his firm could hardly be satisfied with magazine rights only. It was one more reason for him to be suspicious of Simone and of her cousin Julien Benda (who later wrote the great essay, *La Trahison des clercs*). In his bitterness Jacques might well have pointed out that *Le Secret* was about a woman who meddles with the lives of those around her.

Simone in Le Secret

At this stage, with trouble brewing, Fournier went off for a short spell of reserve training at Mirande, where Simone wrote him a cheerful note: 'I hope by now you've had quite enough of being a soldier. The joy of Claude and Péguy when they go off to camp utterly disgusts me. Delighted to know that you're finding it all horrible down there.'

But Simone would not have been pleased if she had known what was in Henri's mind: he saw the Prix Goncourt partly as a means of bringing himself to the attention once again of Yvonne de Quiévrecourt. He had not read *Dominique* for nothing, and still had hopes of winning the lady's love via literary fame. And his boast of bringing her back into his life suddenly looked like coming true. The ground was prepared by Jacques Rivière's young brother Marc, the boy known as Kim or Mowgli. While training to be a naval doctor in the Atlantic town of Rochefort, Marc met Yvonne's husband, also a naval doctor. Then he met Yvonne's sister Jeanne de Quiévrecourt, who promised to help.

So instead of returning directly to Paris after his military interlude, Henri made a detour to Rochefort, and it was ironical that the countryside through which he passed in the train was the setting for *Dominique* itself. Ironical too, that the journey happened on Ascension Day, the eighth anniversary of the day in 1905 when he stood on those steps at the Grand Palais and saw Yvonne de Quiévrecourt for the first time.

A few hours after stepping down from the train he met Jeanne in the Jardin de la Marine. Jeanne had been only thirteen at the time of the brief encounter, but she seemed to have heard all about it and to have found it extremely exciting. She informed Henri that her sister now had *two* children. . . but that a meeting might be arranged.

This duly occurred a fortnight later, again in the Jardin de la Marine. Henri arrived on the Friday (16 May) and when he left the following Monday he bought at the station a small black notebook with red edges in which he noted his impressions (mostly scraps of dialogue) of the Rochefort weekend. Thanks to this notebook, which has been preserved, we can form some idea of what happened.

He met her six times in all: once on the Friday evening of his arrival, again on the Saturday afternoon, and then in the mornings and afternoons of both Sunday and Monday. All

Fournier with his fellow-officers at Mirande, April 1913

the meetings took place in the Jardin de la Marine and on some
occasions her sister was present, and even her mother, who
seems to have been an intrigued spectator.

For the two leading players, however, it must have been
something of an ordeal. Henri was confronting his almost
legendary love in a tête-à-tête between tennis courts, checking
her every word and movement against his memories. She, for
her part, though flattered by his attentions, was resolved to
play the straight bat of Victorian convention. It transpired that
she had been as impressed as he by the original encounter, but
had no present thought of renewing the relationship.

The conversation began extremely cautiously, with an
exchange of banalities, such as the fact that she enjoyed fast
driving. Henri, the racing-buff, was delighted to hear it.
Gradually they returned in memory to that Whit Sunday of
1905. 'What were you writing in the tram?' she asked with
curiosity. 'I've often wondered. I watched you scribbling,
scribbling. What was it?' Henri replied that she might one day
learn. She had also been struck by his extreme youth. Henri,
it will be recalled, had worn his school uniform on the Sunday
in question, and this detail may have scored against him.

Finally he asked if they could be friends, and she said yes,
by all means, he could come to Brest and go on fifteen-mile
walks with her husband – with whom (she said) she was now
on excellent terms, though there had been a time in the past
when things didn't go so well:

> If you'd come three years ago, anything might have been
> possible. I was unhappy and often thought of you. I would
> have written to you if I'd been able. I wasn't getting on at
> all well with my husband. We didn't seem to have a thing
> in common. Since then we've both made concessions and
> forgiven each other. I'm now the happiest of women. It was
> my fault as much as anything: I was a little goose.

As if to emphasize that all her doubts were firmly in the
past and that (to echo Henri's words to Bichet) everything was
no longer possible, she produced her two pretty infants. In his
notebook on the train home Fournier mused incredulously:
'To think she said: I've often thought of you, I nearly wrote
to you!'

It is tempting to speculate on what might have happened if

Henri had re-discovered his Yvonne at the end of his military service in 1909. Despite the information supplied by the detective agency, she did *not* have children at that time, her daughter and son being born in 1910 and 1911 respectively. But Henri's eight years of adoration had surely been for an ideal woman, a dream woman, and never a real one.

And now at last, after the Rochefort conversation, he seems to have accepted the fact himself. And besides. . . with the publication date of *Le Grand Meaulnes* fast approaching. . . had not Yvonne de Quiévrecourt perhaps served her purpose in becoming Yvonne de Galais?

Fournier on a route-march

9 · *Le Sacre du Printemps (1913)*

Ten days after his return from Rochefort – on 29 May 1913 – Henri took Simone to see Gide's own house on the Villa Montmorency estate at Auteuil. She had to leave him sooner than she wished, to see Sarah Bernhardt and Edmond Rostand about a possible part in a revival of Rostand's *La Princesse lointaine*. At this important conference she found herself unable to concentrate and wondered why. Henri, for his part, went home to change for an important event: the first night of *Le Sacre du Printemps* at the newly opened Théâtre des Champs-Elysées. That evening, with Rivière, he witnessed the extraordinary scenes that occurred during and after the Stravinsky-Nijinsky ballet, when the audience divided into two factions and fought a pitched battle.

Protests and derisive laughter had begun with the first bars of the music – only to be followed by counter-protests. While those who were outraged whistled their disgust, the remainder made even more noise cheering and applauding. Soon the elegant mob were shouting and spitting at each other. Faces were slapped in the *fracas*, and in one case cards were exchanged in prelude to a duel. In the ever-increasing uproar Diaghilev's plea from a box to 'let the performance proceed' ('laisser achever le spectacle') went unnoticed. Finally the din was so great that the dancers could no longer hear the music. The house-lights were turned on. But the riot continued. . .

As soon as he could extricate himself Henri rushed round to the Bouffes-Parisiens to give a report to Simone in her dressing-room. They returned to the Quai Debilly and Simone has described the scene as they sat lazily over a midnight snack, occasionally getting up to stroll across to the balcony:

> From the gardens of the Trocadéro there rose the scent of flowers. The tugs and barges of the Seine were asleep, and

the quayside tram had gone home for the night. No car climbed the slope to the rue Boissière and, under a clear sky, the world was bathed in moonlight.

They stood there watching until it became light, when Henri rather suddenly left. Later that day she sent him a *pneumatique* (express letter) recalling the beauty of their nocturnal vigil and adding: 'But why did you leave at dawn?' To which Henri replied with an even shorter *pneu*, promising that a real letter would follow. Finally, after he had cooled down, he wrote the real letter which Simone has confessed 'changed my life', dropping it in at the theatre on Sunday morning, so that she would have it for the matinee: 'It's hard to tell the truth. It's hard to renounce all the charades and enigmas, and I don't do it without anguish. But the fact is I love you. . .' He described how it had happened:

The summer night is ending. The young woman has sent her servants to bed, and the day will soon break. There is but one star remaining, just by the Eiffel Tower. The borders of night are beginning to whiten, but a secret word that waits to be spoken will not be spoken, a kiss will not be given. As the first light of dawn spreads into the streets, everything changes. So it wasn't true, then, after all? The young woman on the balcony wonders if she was mistaken, and an absurd young man rushes off through the empty streets with an overwhelming desire to weep.

He recalls an incident earlier that day when, in similar fashion, he had failed to act:

Do you remember, near the gate of Villa Montmorency, you turned round rather abruptly with the funny awkward movement of someone not much used to walking. [or should one perhaps blame Poiret's new slim-line skirt?] and you were suddenly very close to me, small and thoughtful and worried. . .?

He had long imagined himself writing this letter (he told her). He had planned it to be a deliciously rambling letter, written very slowly but – as things had turned out – it was having to be written in haste: 'Just now in the street, on this rainy summer morning, someone is playing a very inexpert flute. And in the *salon* next door they're talking loudly of everyday matters.' Against this background he tries to recall the first moment he was in love: it was an evening when he found himself saying: 'It's nine o'clock. . . she's at the theatre. . . she's now on stage. . . it's the interval. . . she's taking off her make-up. . . she's going home.'

> Where I love you most is at the theatre. That's where you seem to me most alone – and most attentive to all I say. That's where I'm nearest you. What a wrench it is for me to let you go at the end of the intervals! And how I love the looks you give me, so serenely tender and happy, when other people are there!
>
> When I came home on the night of *Le Sacre* I realized that something in my life had ended for ever, and something else was beginning: something wonderful and beautiful, which might also be terrible and perhaps fatal [. . .] There are a number of solutions: you may perhaps reject me completely and I shall leave at once. The book [*Brest: port transatlantique*] is almost finished, so that would be an excuse. Or else you will just ignore this letter of mine. You will burn it, but still remain my friend, while I shall return to being my well-behaved and silent self. Or else – my gentle friend, my love, my tender love – you will respond to me. And I, who have never even kissed your hand, will take you in my arms. . .

From another letter dating from about this time (early June 1913), Simone has published the following:

> On my way home, ten minute after leaving you. I'm yours distractedly. *Eperdument!* Even the word is yours. I'm suffocating with a happiness that is still growing. Only now can I realize the full extent of it. Every moment it constrains my heart a little more. Shall I be able to stand it without going mad, or shouting, or dying?

On 15 June 1913 *Le Secret* ended the first part of its run, and on 23 June transferred for a week to the New Theatre, London, in connection with the special visit to England of President Poincaré. On this occasion the *Illustrated London News* described Simone as 'a seductive little Iago in petticoats' but she wrote to Henri only of her frustration, and how she was reduced to kicking the London furniture, to the amusement of her dresser. On hearing that he was playing tennis, she asks him wistfully if tennis can so easily replace the Boulevard Arago, the latter being the address of a flat they had rented for their rendezvous, and therefore eloquent shorthand for love. Next day she asks for forgiveness for her 'sad letter of yesterday, but I saw you in your tennis outfit, all happy and carefree, while I was here miserable.' She would have been even more miserable if she had known that Henri was indulging in his dangerous new passion for aviation – a fact he reveals in a note to Marguerite Audoux on 28 June ('I therefore can't spend the hour in your little flat that I had promised myself.')

Next day Simone was back in Paris, and on the first of July *Le Grand Meaulnes* began its serialization in the *Nouvelle Revue Française* where it ran in five monthly issues, closing on the first of November. The book-rights had gone to Emile-Paul and Jacques was bitterly disappointed. During the month of July Henri spent long weekends at Trie. He wrote from there on the twelfth in an obvious attempt to clear the air and improve their relations:

> My dear old impossible Jacques, I want to tell you something: happiness is a terribly difficult thing to bear, especially if it isn't the kind of happiness you've been brought up to expect. And on that point I have nothing more to say.

He went on to remark that he had just been out for a walk and had been breathing country air for the first time since his arrival, this being an allusion to Simone's well-known aversion to walking.

> And now, at 9 p.m. I'm in the small drawing room, where Claude's playing the piano and Simone is stretched out in the shadows on a big divan. She's just asked me who I'm writing to and sends her love. I've been thinking of you both and Jacqueline this evening. I've been thinking that, if my destiny hadn't taken this turning, we'd be together now – because I have never stopped loving all three of you very deeply.

In a postscript he mentions that he is awaiting proofs for the August *NRF*. This was the number from which Paris learnt for the first time of 'Le Domaine Mystérieux' and 'La Fête Étrange'. In a second postscript he says: 'Simone has suggested

5ᵉ ANNÉE. Nᵒ 55.   1ᵉʳ JUILLET 1913

LA NOUVELLE
REVUE FRANÇAISE

SOMMAIRE :

LA NOUVELLE REVUE FRANÇAISE
35 & 37, RUE MADAME, PARIS

that I should do a stage adaptation of one of Stevenson's novels, which she will play 3,000 times in America and make our fortune!'

Jacques and Isabelle were staying at the time with the Gaston Gallimards near Deauville, where Simone was scheduled to give a special performance of *Le Secret* at the Casino. There was some question of Henri going along too, but he was passing through a difficult period, pulled in many different directions. He was tempted to go on another of Péguy's walks to Chartres, but his proofs were late and he felt in duty bound to stay on call. In the end he went to Paris and brooded over . . . Yvonne de Quiévrecourt! His mind was in a tumult, occasioned no doubt by the events of the past three months: first the Rochefort encounter, followed by *Le Sacre* and those more personal rites of spring that engulfed him in Paris in June. He asked Péguy and Jacques successively to advise him about Simone, but neither was inclined to commit himself. Finally he called Simone to Paris and confronted her with the news that he had recently seen Yvonne de Quiévrecourt. Her instinct, not unreasonably, was to leave at once – whereupon he had some sort of fit, and writhed on the floor of his room at rue Cassini. The way she puts it is this: 'He fell to the parquet and then thrashed about, shouting, as if he were being devoured by flames.' After the concierge had come up to see what the trouble was, the two lovers gaily hailed an open cab and drove to the Quai Debilly. where they consoled themselves in private for the next two days.

Simone now left for Cambo with Claude, while Henri went to La Chapelle alone. Because of the presence of Claude at Cambo, Henri's letters were for a time merely 'lettres officielles', a series of amusing snippets. Here is an extract from one reproduced facsimile in Jean Bastaire's *Alain-Fournier où la Tentation de la jeunesse* (1964), page 162:

I've been reading Flaubert's letters and they're interesting enough, but what a sad period it was, that of de Goncourt, Maupassant and Daudet, all those short-sighted individuals who sat down to record, without hope or joy, the world as they believed it to be. What a life without depth was theirs! Whereas today we have the exquisite Stevenson, setting out on a donkey one evening to discover the Cevennes. How

fresh everything is today! How good to breathe and be alive!
Ah that adorable *Travels with a donkey*! It's out of print,
but I must find you a copy.

Indeed, it was with some justification that Mme Simone once
called Fournier 'the faithful friend of Stevenson'. With its many
short chapters and anecdotal chapter-headings, *Le Grand
Meaulnes* bears a slight formal resemblance to *Treasure Island*,
but even more to *Kidnapped*. At the beginning of the latter
book, Chapter One is titled 'I set off upon my journey to the
House of Shaws', the hero being a sixteen-year-old son of a
schoolmaster and the object of his quest a country château.
When he comes upon it at sundown, it seems to be a kind of
ruin, the windows unglazed, while bats fly in and out. He
awakens next day in a fine dilapidated room, a great chamber
hung with stamped leather, which ten or twenty years ago
must have been a pleasant place. Does this seem vaguely familiar to amateurs of the Lost Domain? But Fournier never hid
his admiration for English adventure stories, nor his urge to
emulate them. In fact, this very same year, on 16 February,
he had proclaimed in the Paris paper *L'Intransigeant*: 'Goodbye, Symbolism! We're going to show the English that we,
too, can tell stories.' True, he did not quite deliver the goods,
for Symbolism could not be seen off as easily as that. It is
touching all the same to note his intention to write a 'ripping
yarn' à l'anglaise.

At last Claude departed on his various errands and the letters
change in tone. They become more abandoned, but also more
anguished:

> Pauline darling, Jacques is hurrying me to correct proofs,
> so I haven't much time. Dearest Pauline, my beautiful child,
> I'm afraid the letter you got from me on Monday must have
> made you sad. My love, be sure of this one thing: whatever
> happened before, it's only our love that counts now. I adore
> you.

Pauline (her real name) had indeed been depressed by the
Monday letter, whatever it may have said. She therefore summoned Henri by telegram to Cambo and he responded with
alacrity. In order to reach Bayonne (her nearest station) he
had first to proceed to Paris. While changing trains at Bourges
he sent Jacques a last-minute correction for the September

NRF, with a reference to the oath-swearing scene (*LGM*, p. 121), which originally took place 'dans la pénombre *de la tombée* de la nuit.' KILL 'THE FALL OF NIGHT', he wired grandly, reflecting afterwards that it was the sort of telegram that God Himself might write. (In the way of the world, however, his instructions were ignored until the 1971 Livre de Poche edition.)

Meanwhile Simone had driven in from Cambo to meet him but, arriving early, was killing time on the beach at Biarritz, one eye on the Casino clock. Their reunion was joyous, and the fortnight that followed at the Villa Souberbielle one of the happiest periods of Fournier's life. Being mostly alone with her, he had less cause than usual to be jealous. The house, too, was simple and countrified, which reassured him. Even the dreaded neighbour Edmond Rostand – Simone had played the Pheasant in his *Chantecler* – did not materialize to interrupt their sweet solitude. Claude and the chauffeur being otherwise engaged, they made many delightful excursions in a horse-drawn carriage to Basque villages – Itxassou for instance. A visit was even made to the Orthez home of the poet Francis Jammes. (This would have been a dream come true in Fournier's youth but, as happens in life, it happened too late.)

'When will you come and see *my* country?' Henri had written from La Chapelle – and Simone decided now to accept the invitation. On 11 September she and Henri left Cambo in the big Delaunay motor-car driven by Claude. First stop was an unfortunate courtesy call on Jacques' family at Cenon. The welcome in that otherwise pleasant stronghold was strained, Simone being not only an actress but a divorced one.

All went surprisingly well, on the other hand, at La Chapelle. Both Mme Fournier and Maman-Barthe felt at home with Simone, and the only embarrassed person (understandably) was Claude, who soon left on urgent business to Paris. The couple then had five days alone together (14-18 September), which they called ever afterwards 'nos noces' ('our honeymoon'). The only casualty was Henri's proof-reading (both for the *NRF* and Émile-Paul) which he had unavoidably to delegate.

Claude at length returned for his wife and drove her back to Paris on 19 September. The two long letters that Henri sent

Simone, on the 20th and 21st, give some idea of 'nos noces' at La Chapelle:

> Trying to begin life again without you is terrible. Yesterday I was unwise enough to go into our room. Your scent was still in the air. And on the little table I found a blonde hair and a pin. During those five days, each time I crept furtively into the room I'd hear you say, 'Close the door and come and kiss me.' And I swear to you I seemed to hear it this time too! How sad it is at night no longer to hear my love preparing herself for love! How hard to be woken no more at dawn by the steps of the men going to work, whilst our room has remained mysteriously illuminated all night!
>
> At last I really know you. I know you exactly as you are and how you live, my young and gay, simple and funny, adorable girl. I've seen you crouching in front of the fire, poking the embers. I've seen you at table, turning round to throw bread to the chickens as they come in from the rain. There's not a gesture or word or smile of yours that isn't as close to my heart as that bend in the road which I showed you. Till Tuesday, my adored darling, my child, my woman.

The next day he wrote:

> My darling Pauline, I thought of this: I'll be alone in Paris, My mother won't be coming back till later – my father's not there – and I'll send away the maid. So you can come to me there, in 'that little room where we were so unhappy' but where this time we'll be happy (till our own place is ready). I know I'm going to see you the day after tomorrow, but sometimes I wonder if I'm ever going to see you again as I have done here. Shall I ever be able to hold you close at any hour of the day, and snuggle my head into your neck and adored hair?
>
> I am thinking of your beauty and your grace which seduced everyone here. I think of the red nightdress you put on to wait for me at night. I think of our whispered conversations, our kisses and smothered laughs. I think of those five days of hidden love, when it seemed we used up all the happiness that was due to us on earth. My love, my love, tell me that it's not finished, that it's not all over.

The *reprise* of *Le Secret* took place on 18 October, when the

Comoedia critic proclaimed that Simone was now more moving than ever, but a few scattered notes in a 1913 diary show
that Fournier himself had worries. The Bouffes-Parisiens had
been redecorated by Henry Bernstein, who was now lessee of
the theatre as well as author of the play, a concentration of
power which Henri Fournier resented. But it wasn't only the
individual personalities surrounding Simone that irked Henri
– the whole atmosphere of the Paris stage now ruffled the
feathers of this country boy. It was the theatre in general that
he was jealous of – as being the prime culprit in a conspiracy
which prevented him having Simone to himself. Although
there were moments when he seemed to be as stage-struck as
the next man, his main efforts from now on were to persuade
Simone to retire from acting altogether and devote the rest of
her life to raising a family. It does not seem to have crossed
his mind that such an idea might be unreasonable or even pre-
sumptuous.

Their small flat in 'B.A.' (Boulevard Arago) consisted of
two floor rooms at No. 97, on the south side, behind the
young double row of young chestnut trees near the place
Denfert-Rochereau. The door of their apartment was
immediately to the left as you entered the building, that is even
before you reached the concierge's *loge.* The flat had originally
been let furnished to them in June, but Simone was not happy
with the furnishings and the landlord had agreed to remove
them as soon as possible. That time had now arrived. Henri
wrote to Jacques on 19 September, just before leaving La
Chapelle, for advice about selling the few shares he owned.
He had insisted on going halves in the decorating costs and,
in view of Simone's other commitments, he would also be the
one to supervise operations. On 26 October the landlord gave
the word, but the diary indicates that Simone's reaction was
not enthusiastic:
'When I tell her about Arago, she says she feels sad and tired.
Downstairs I run into Bernstein with his eternal scarf.' Next
day: 'I go round to Arago. It's moving day. Straw everywhere.
I take some measurements.' On 4 November: 'Arago 2.30
p.m. I wait by the fire. Her high heels in the rain and enormous
hat. Our home. She's still not well.'

Le Grand Meaulnes was published in book form just as the

final instalment (November) appeared in the *NRF*. A fortnight later *Le Secret* closed (perhaps because of Simone's poor health) and she was now able to concentrate her still considerable energies on getting Henri the Prix Goncourt. Largely due to her efforts, Alain-Fournier was soon favourite. Photographs by the most fashionable photographers were made available to the press, and if the one by Manuel had an uncanny resemblance to the Keats portrait, it was no accident, the session being supervised by Simone.

On the day of the voting (3 December) a luncheon party was arranged at the Quai Debilly. It was planned that Claude would receive the result by telephone in another room. If he rejoined the party with empty hands (ready to applaud) it would mean success. In the event Claude came in carrying a piece of rolled-up paper, and Simone proceeded to break the news to her protégé as gently as she could.

The voting had gone to eleven rounds, with the usual finessing between rival supporters. *Le Grand Meaulnes* had failed to win the prize by the merest whisker. Such a controversial result, however, with its suggestion that justice had not been done, was excellent publicity. The reviews were generally good and Fournier became overnight the talk of the town. It was word of mouth, however, passed on by one reader to another, that eventually made the book a world-wide bestseller, translated into more than thirty languages. As for the novel that actually won the Prix Goncourt for 1913 – *Le Peuple de la Mer* by Marc Elder – it has never been heard of since.

A copy of *Le Grand Meaulnes* flamboyantly inscribed by the author to 'Madame Yvonne Brochet de Quiévrecourt, Comtesse de Vaugrigneuse', will certainly have pleased that lady, for whom protocol always counted. She died on 29 December 1964, having represented, for her generation, what the Blue Flower of Novalis had meant to an earlier one: the idea that 'somewhere, but always out of reach, there exists a happiness which ravishes the soul.'[1]

[1] The quotation is from Alan Pryce-Jones's introduction to *The Lost Domain* (OUP, 1959) – Frank Davison's excellent translation of *LGM*, which is now in Penguin under the original French title; also re-issued by OUP (1986) with an Afterword by John Fowles.

The Candidate for the Prix Goncourt, by Manuel

10 · *The curtain falls (1914)*

One would have wished for Alain-Fournier, author of the brilliant bestseller *Le Grand Meaulnes*, a joyous life in prospect, illustrated perhaps by the evocative photographs of Lartigue, with bevies of elegant women and graceful girls amidst the first aeroplanes and vintage cars. And, certainly, when he and Simone fell in love on the first night of *Le Sacre Du Printemps*, what could have been more appropriate? And when he became Hon. Sec. of the literary rugby team (the Club Sportif de la Jeunesse Littéraire) with Péguy for President and an *équipe* including Giraudoux, MacOrlan, Gallimard, Rivière and himself, it had just the right carefree touch, redolent of the Douanier Rousseau's 'Football players' of 1908. Notices of fixtures were jokily countersigned by Augustin Meaulnes and Frantz de Galais: everything was going to plan. . .

There was nothing in all this to signal the implacable dénouement: the bullet in the head in a muddy wood on the German frontier.

He had now less than a year to live, and one would like to report that he strode through those last months like a king. It would not be true: like any lovers, he and Simone had their good times and less good times, beginning (in the first months of 1914) with the latter.

Gérard de Nerval once said that 'nothing is more dangerous for someone of a dreamy disposition than to fall in love with an actress'. She is a special sort of being: to maintain the momentum and glamour of stardom is tough and tiring work, the endless intrigue for parts and publicity being no routine for weaklings. Fournier seems never to have made allowances for the immense nervous energy that an actress has to expend.

After the close of *Le Secret* Simone began rehearsals for a new rôle in another play especially written for her: François de Curel's *La Danse devant le Miroir*, which opened at the

Ambigu on 17 January. It was about a couple who torture themselves, each seeking to satisfy the idea which he/she has conceived of the other: each thus becoming the mirror of the other's wish, and so untrue to self. *Comoedia* thought she had 'never been so beautiful', but the play itself failed to please and, when it was withdrawn on 19 February, it was reported that the star was ill. Nonetheless she was already rehearsing for Henri Lavedan's *Le Pétard*, which opened on the first of April but ended, so far as Simone was concerned, on the eleventh. She was ill again.

These facts must be borne in mind when studying Fournier's Green Agenda, a book bound in leather of that colour and containing sketchy, abbreviated, often enigmatic, pencil scribbles describing his day-to-day concerns from 13 January to 19 April. Most of the entries have been published in Isabelle Rivière's major work, *Vie et Passion d'Alain-Fournier* (pp. 286-336), though not chronologically. What follows is a small selection.

On 23 January he quotes Simone as saying, 'Oh for a fortnight in the country with you!' and on 25 January: 'Three weeks alone with you snuggling into my back, that's all I ask!' But next day he complains that she has put off coming to B.A. from 3.30 to 4.30 and then didn't arrive till 5.30. He laments his long wait in the dark room, while night fell bleakly on the drizzle and thaw outside. 'She thinks of nothing but her work and her rôle,' he says on 28 January. That is a fairly typical sequence. The diary continues as follows:

Thurs 29th – It's not just that I want her. I need her to live. Today she came while I was out. When I arrived, I found the armchair pulled up to the fire and a hairpin on the floor.
Sat 31st – My terrible dream. Her sunken face – the wound – the obscene twist of the mouth and eyes as she looks up at the astonished waiter. . .
Sun 1st Feb – 'Try at least to sit still on your chair'
Sun 8th – She wants to take me to America for six months, and she doesn't care who knows it.
Mon 9th – At midnight she wants to go to the Bois, then changes her mind, then forgets she's changed her mind.
Tues 10th – She arrives just when the waiting's become unbearable. I dash out to buy her milk.

Sat 14th – 'Even three years from now, you'd not be in a position to prevent people saying: "He married her for her money."'

Sun 15th – 'This is the first day we haven't quarrelled.'

Mon 16th – An immense tenderness for my sick love.

Tues 17th – Not even a kiss. 'It's as if you asked for tenderness from a woman who's sea-sick.' Bernstein's shady financiers as the reality of life!

Wed 18th – 'Your pity always takes the same form: a hand on my breast.'

Thurs 19th – No nestling up, just a sad kiss.

Sat 21st – Her dear sweet face, when she's really attentive to what you say. Her expression suddenly so serious that it makes you smile.

Sat 7th March – Bernstein, Curel, Lavedan.

Mon 9th – Not even a kiss in the neck like Lavedan.

Tues 10th – A woman that men don't respect. (Bernstein, Lavedan, Roux, Curel.)

Thurs 12th – We've lost the mischievousness we used to have: her comb in my pocket, the lighted lamp, the upturned inkwell. [At this point Claude takes Henri to the South of France on a weekend of electioneering.]

Sun 15th – Not much for a man just back from a long journey: a whispered word outside the door, a hand furtively pressed. The three of us go walking in the Bois. The imprudent kiss. [A day after 'the imprudent kiss' a politico-media-sex scandal rocks Paris: Mme Caillaux, wife of the Finance Minister, shoots dead in his office the editor of *Le Figaro*, Gaston Calmette.]

Thurs 19th – That charming, feminine, white face with the hair drawn back – just for a second in the mirror.

Sat 21st – More praise for Bernstein. His courage.

Sun 22nd – 'I've hardly an atom of life left in me.' She's ill and tired and upset. But why take it out on our love?

Mon 23rd – Her talk about Donnay is not what I care to hear. 'Those things that recall your youth, it makes me sad to think about them.' – 'Then don't!'

Tues 24th – A conversation about Bernstein.

Thurs 26th – The most charmingly insidious face in the world.

Mon 30th – Her assumption that my caresses are a breach of trust. . .

Tues 31st – . . . while hers can settle anything!

Wed 1st April – The first night [of Lavedan's *Le Pétard*]. The aquiline nose and high shoulders, the arms at right angles as in an Egyptian frieze. How could one ever deprive oneself of such a countenance! That tender, pearly, lustrous look – like something about to blossom, or to emerge from a chrysalis or from the depths of a wave.

Fri 10th – She arrives quite exalted with the thought of playing [Bernstein's] *Judith*. She sees no difference in the quality of one work and another. Her flood of words to describe the projects of de Croisset!

Sat 11th – Bernstein and *Judith*.

Mon 13th – She's in pain. Her hand in mine. 'It helps when you're there.'

Tues 14th – The way she talks about men with Mme X when they're alone together.

Sat 18th – 'I'll never have children, even if you begged me. . .' In the library I come across a line of poetry: 'Alas for the happiness I believed possible!' ('Hélas! tout ce bonheur que je croyais possible!')

And so ends the Green Agenda. 'At this point,' writes Isabelle Rivière, 'there occurred a tragedy of which I cannot speak but which – for Henri – was the most terrible heart-break his life could ever know.' Henri's own reaction can be read in his letter to Simone of 21 April:

> There are a thousand tendernesses that I couldn't say to you yesterday. . . I still see your beautiful, suffering face and am repeating to myself, with a passion and sincerity you can't imagine, the poor frightened words you spoke. I am dying of the desire to take you in my arms again, to hold you close to me, my darling who has suffered so much, my little child who is so sick [. . .] Pacing up and down your room yesterday, I couldn't even give you my hand to calm you or help the pain because. . . *the door was open!* I could say nothing to you, do nothing for you. Yet to stop your suffering I would have given the last drop of my blood.

The open door, referred to here, harks back to *Pelléas* (Act III, Scene 4), which is not in any way to question his sincerity. . .

On 26 April Claude was defeated in his attempt to enter

parliament for Béziers and, since the book on Brest had now been completed anyway and he no longer needed a secretary, Simone and Henri had to find some other excuse (in the eyes of the world) for staying together. They decided it would be the play *La Maison dans la forêt*.

On the first day of collaboration at Trie, Simone placed a symbolic ribbon and flower in an envelope ('un ruban et une fleur') by way of marking the occasion. But Mme Rivière, who found the envelope among his papers, bearing indeed the words, 'first day of collaboration', claimed that it contained only a broken suspender ('une jarretelle cassée'). The symbolic suspender (or was it a rose?) is beautifully expressive of the relations between these two eminent ladies, Mme Rivière viewing with scepticism of course, the idea of a literary collaboration. In this, perhaps, she was a little unfair since Mme Simone in later years had much to do with the rise to fame of the playwright Stève Passeur and, even in 1914, her knowledge of stagecraft could have been a boon to any aspiring dramatist. (She also became a famous novelist in her own right, her best-known book being *Jours de Colère*.)

As it happens, the play was never finished, because Fournier's publisher now began clamouring for another novel. And the novel – *Colombe Blanchet* – was not finished, either, because life at Trie was too delicious. The two months spent there in the summer of 1914 represented the happiest period of Fournier's brief life. He at last had Simone to himself again, away from all her Paris preoccupations, and they were able to resume the honeymoon ('nos noces') begun at La Chapelle the previous year.

'If the weather was fine,' said Simone, 'we installed ourselves under the plane tree, where I'd be reading quietly by his side. After two or three hours he'd push aside pen and paper and sweep me into a great dance round the lawn.' Henri told Lhote that their time was divided between literary and rural pursuits: five hours on the novel, followed by raking hay under the chestnut trees or tending the bees. 'We're alone every day except Sunday,' he told Isabelle, for Claude had departed on a private mission to Vittel. 'It's Happy Valley – a landscape either blue or gold, according to whether we're in the shade or sun. A landscape with geraniums, lawns, a stream and a little wood with two benches – one for happy days and one for sad, but it's some time since we used the latter.'

He was thinking, perhaps, of the day when they had discovered Maurice Donnay in the church at Gisors – which seemed such a coincidence that it had brought all Henri's jealous instincts rushing to the surface. But most of the time they were idyllically happy: to the point of convincing sceptics like Jacques and Isabelle that the relationship might have a future after all. 'The weather's great,' wrote Henri in the last-but-one letter he ever wrote to Jacques. 'By which I mean there's been a prodigious thunderstorm going on since midday, which terrifies one of us, delights the other and lays waste the garden.'

On their way to Cambo in the middle of July, they decided to see Jacques and Isabelle, whom they invited to lunch at the Hôtel de France in Bordeaux. Judging from Isabelle's subsequent graphic description, this must have been an extremely uncomfortable lunch party – and Jacques certainly shared her feelings. Simone, it seems, gave a most remarkable performance – that of a famous actress indulging herself – while Isabelle contemplated her antics with lofty disdain. Between these two personalities Henri had the minor rôle of sitting still and looking sheepish, 'like a little boy with his governess,' said Isabelle.

Mme Rivière then gives an alarming account – almost worthy of Céline – of how Simone, in the manner of a brisk sergeant-major, lined up the entire hotel staff in the lobby after lunch. Slapping down a huge pile of five-franc pieces on the reception counter, she proceeded to drop a coin into each outstretched hand, receiving a bow or a curtsey in exchange, till finally the largesse was exhausted. She then spun neatly on her heel and flounced out of the hotel, followed by her maid Marie-Louise and her secretary Henri, to join her chauffeur Jossien at the bottom of the steps. If this scene happened as stated, it is a remarkable example of how things were done in the grand hotels of pre-war France.

What Jacques called 'that ghastly meeting' ('cette horrible entrevue') came to an all too fitting climax. Having promised to drop off the Rivières at an address in Bordeaux, Henri and Simone forgot the arrangement, leaving Jacques and Isabelle standing speechless on the hotel steps as the big Delaunay convertible vanished in a cloud of dust. Their only consolation was a card next day from Henri: 'My dears, we were simply furious with you. Why on earth didn't you remind us you wanted a lift? We never gave it a thought till we were the other side of Bordeaux. You really are too silly.' It was the last time Jacques and Isabelle ever saw Alain-Fournier.

The Author in his Study, rue Cassini, by Dornac

The curtain was about to go up on the last act: Henri and Simone had barely a week to enjoy the delights of Cambo. War was already in the air, and Henri just had time to turn down an offer from Paris to become an English interpreter. In doing so he sealed his fate.

The couple were in Bayonne on the first of August when the church bells rang out for the mobilization. From the Grand Café du Port he sent a quick note to Isabelle at Cenon. By midnight he and Simone were at Mirande – Lieutenant Fournier of the 288th Regiment already resplendent in his black and gold uniform. The little town was brimming with soldiers. After a last night together, Simone departed. But she left a solemn letter, in which she promised to marry him after the war and to become a practising Catholic. In the noise and bustle of Mirande's Café de Bordeaux, surrounded by so many people he could hardly think, he asked for writing paper and solemnly thanked his 'young Jewish wife with whom I shall present myself before God.' He said that he had guessed what was in the letter the moment he saw it, and nothing could have moved him more. 'I am thinking of your letter. . . I shall never stop thinking of it.' When he had gone back to their room to collect his things (he said), he seemed to hear her calling his name. And when he had said goodbye to her: 'I felt it was you they were sending off to war.'

Next day (4 August) he informed Isabelle of their decision to marry, and also that they were trying to get Fournier's parents to Cambo. He prayed that his sister and future wife would get on well together ('Je voudrais que tu l'aimes beaucoup'). He was again writing from the first floor of the Café de Bordeaux at Mirande, and described the scene in the Place d'Astarac below, where the town crier had just announced England's declaration of war.

On Thursday 6 August Simone made a surprise return to Mirande, in order to be with Henri till the very last minute. On Saturday the Fournier parents, too, arrived, having come via Cenon and Marmande, where they had seen Isabelle and Jacques respectively, Jacques having joined his regiment, the 220th.

Next day, at four in the morning, Henri marched off with his men to the nearby town of Auch, followed soon by Simone and the parents, who remained at Auch till Wednesday evening, when the soldiers entrained for the front. While a band played the Marseillaise, amid tears and jubilation, the train moved off, and Simone tells how she galloped along the platform, like a wild thing ('courant, galopant, égarée') as it gathered speed. To which Isabelle coolly replies that such an athletic performance would have been difficult ('a de quoi surprendre') since the platform was jam-packed with waving relatives.

In the days that followed, news of Henri's progress towards the front – a crawling train journey of five-hundred miles in four days – was conveyed home by a series of postcards: to Simone and the parents at Cambo, to Isabelle at Cenon. By a strange coincidence Henri Fournier's train crept across France immediately behind that of Jacques Rivière so that Jacques could write:

> We passed the same stations, where the women pinned holy medals on our chests, while in the same fields the peasants removed their hats as we passed, as if they recognized the train already as a hearse. We heard the Marseillaise bawled out in similar accents and with similar garlicky breaths, since we were both in Gascon regiments.

A postcard view of Périgueux on the 13th enjoined Isabelle once more to 'write to Pauline, who'll write to you'. By Friday evening the train had reached Bourges, and Isabelle's postcard view was of their beloved Cher, with the message: 'Have just been listening to some charming children speaking the best French in France'. Another two days brought them to Suippes (east of Reims) where they disembarked on Sunday night (16 August). Next day they started marching to the front.

On or about 18 August Henri sent a card to Isabelle saying, 'We're getting near, we can hear gunfire.' He added that 'the *Grand Meaulnes* knife' (*LGM* p. 47) which Isabelle had given him, and for which he had paid her the traditional *sou*, was already proving indispensable.

It was also now that he wrote to Marguerite Audoux, asking her to destroy certain letters he had written her about Yvonne de Quiévrecourt:

> There is now someone else, whom I love more than anyone in the world, and I don't want to risk those letters falling into her hands – in case she might think that my immense

love for her was in any way shared or restricted. I count on you absolutely to burn those letters.

On 20 August he sent a long, rambling and very strange letter to Simone herself, in which he recounts a dream that has disturbed him:

> You were in mourning for Claude's parents, and for some reason it was advisable for you to wash your hands of me. I couldn't understand why you would do such a horrible thing [. . .] In the end you sat down and wrote me a letter, which was bordered with black and brought to me by Alfred Benoist [a childhood friend who had been drowned]. The letter was addressed 'For Alban', which is one of my Christian names never used – I wondered if you had used it out of tenderness or with irony. I decided that the letter must be calling me back to you, and that your love had proved stronger than self-interest. But it was only about some job you had found for me on *Paris-Journal*!

He begs her not to do ambulance work:

> I don't want you to mix with those people, they're like crows: all they know of battles is the aftermath, the corpses. They're only good for cutting people's limbs off. You know that I never admired doctors. I despise their short-sighted materialism, which can't see farther than tendons and veins and grey matter. I'd hate, Pauline, for you to be on that side of life, while we here are on the other.

He asks her not to send telegrams, but always letters. 'A telegram deprives me of your handwriting.' When he is depressed, it is only 'those letters on blue notepaper' that revive him. He also wants a photograph: 'even if it's only by one of those five-sou merchants. Please give me this happiness and consider that there are hundreds of pictures of you in magazines, yet I haven't got your angel's features even on a snipped-out scrap of newsprint.'

> When shall I hear you say, 'Come closer, closer still'? All those things come back to me in waves, like vague memories of life on another planet. The other day I was looking for Cambo on a map of France in the officers' mess, and I suddenly realized that that little name, in the lower left-hand

corner, was the name of my native land.

Henri's and Jacques' regiments (the 288th and 220th) were in adjoining sectors, and soon both were in the thick of the fighting: they were holding the hinge on which the whole front depended. At Etain (north-east of Verdun) on 24 August Henri had his field-glasses smashed at his side; and in the same engagement Jacques went missing. In a letter to Simone dated 3 September, Henri describes his desperate efforts to find out what had become of his friend. (As it happened, Jacques had been taken prisoner, but Henri was never to know this.)

> About Jacques, this is all I know. He must have been wounded at Etain. Was he picked up by our side? Is he in a field hospital somewhere? Or was he captured by the Uhlans? I just don't know. Unluckily, his regiment couldn't hold out till night, as we did. That's what saved us, but Jacques's lot had to retreat at five in the afternoon, in broad daylight [. . .] There's a man here who was with him during the retreat but later lost sight of him. . . The shells were still falling. . . Perhaps he reached another sector. . . Oh God, I pray that he wasn't killed that night! I pray to God that he wasn't killed!

But in the northern part of the front, the Germans had broken through and were advancing on Paris with alarming speed. The Government had retired to Bordeaux, and it was to Bordeaux that Mme Simone now also made her way, accompanied by Mme Fournier. (M. Fournier had been left at Cambo to hold the fort.) Simone wished above all to be near the source of news, and she was well placed to get it from Government circles, being on excellent terms with Aristide Briand and other luminaries. Ever resourceful – she even made a dash to Paris to rescue a small Chardin – Simone was unsuccessful, however, when she tried to make her headquarters at Cenon. Even though they suspected nothing yet of her affair with Henri, she was still an actress and a divorced woman. So Simone found lodgings for Mme Fournier and herself in the centre of the city. They consoled themselves with their own company.

By the beginning of September the Germans were closing in on Paris and all seemed lost. Then, on 5 September, began the miracle: the Battle of the Marne, the counter-attack which, within a week, threw the Germans back north of the Soissons-Reims line. In retrospect it seems almost inevitable that Péguy's name should be linked with the battle that saved France. He was killed on that very first day (5 September) and the spot where he fell – Villeroy – was only fourteen miles from Paris. And it was Péguy's comrade-in-arms, the playboy Claude Casimir-Perier, who sent condolences to the widow in a letter which is a model of its kind, moving in its simplicity: 'We buried him in a village cemetery. After the war, Madame, I will take you there.' But it was not to be: Claude himself was killed in March 1915.

In the meantime Fournier's unit – still on the German frontier, 130 miles to the east – held firm. The victory of the Marne was proclaimed on 13 September, and on the same day, to Simone's joy, a telegram arrived from Henri. He had been made a liaison officer, attached to Brigade HQ, and he had got this safer posting, not through any influence, but because of his fluent English and good horsemanship. Alas, it lasted but a week: on 21 September he was transferred back to his own regiment. And on 22 September he was shot down while leading his company in the woods of Saint-Rémy, between Metz and Verdun.

In one of his last letters to Simone he had said: 'There's a wonderful book to be written about this war, if God will help me.' And in the last letter of all, written on 19 September, he greeted his 'wife-to-be' with the words: 'Here's to the happiness that awaits us and the children we shall have!'

When Simone received the letter Fournier was already dead, his brief life cut off (like Laforgue's) at twenty-seven.

As for Simone herself, she died only last year (on 18 October 1985) in a nursing home on the Basque Coast, after one of the longest lives recorded this century: she was 108.

Le Secrétaire,

H.A. FOURNIER.

Vu et approuvé Augustin meaulnes

Franh de Galais

APPENDIX

Alain-Fournier and T. S. Eliot

As we go to press a letter has come to light, written by Alain-Fournier to T. S. Eliot. Communicated by Mrs Valerie Eliot to Alain Rivière, it was originally addressed to Eliot during his brief visit to Germany in the summer of 1911, before his return to the States in September. The complete French text, with a commentary by Stuart Barr, will be found in the *Bulletin des Amis de Jacques Rivière et d'Alain-Fournier*, no. 39 (1986), but further textual publication is reserved for the forthcoming Eliot *Correspondence*, Vol. I. We are therefore restricted here to a paraphrase of the contents.

Alain-Fournier thanks Eliot (on 25 July) for sending him a list of English books to read — and for the gift of one in particular by [John] Ford [the seventeenth century dramatist], which he found full of passion and tragic beauty. He has been in the country for a few days,[1] during which he finished Stevenson's *Catriona*, a book which delighted him, full of mad adventures presented with great subtlety and skill. He is also reading Conrad's *Typhoon*, which Eliot had recommended, and plans to buy *Youth*.

His philosophy pupil Dubois has passed the baccalauréat exam with flying colours, thanks precisely to sensational marks in philosophy, thus proving that Fournier is as good a teacher as he is a columnist.[2] He will not presume, however, to give any more philosophy lessons to Eliot. Only French ones.[3]

He expresses interest in Eliot's views on the Germans. He himself was once an internationalist, but now is prepared to march against them — and most Frenchmen feel the same.

He has taken the book parcels to the rue Saint-Jacques but found that Eliot had already left.[4] He regrets he will not be in Paris in September, having to go to Mirande for a spell of Army training.

Finally he announces a piece of his to appear in the *NRF* for 1st September.[5]

1. Fournier had been on a week's holiday from *Paris-Journal,* staying with Maman Barthe, his maternal grandmother, in the house at La Chapelle d'Angillon where he was born on 3 October 1886.

2. The delighted Dubois rewarded Fournier on this occasion with a pair of cuff-links. Like Fournier he was to die in the war.

3. The implication that Fournier had at some time given Eliot philosophy lessons is developed at length by Stuart Barr in his interesting 4,500-word commentary. Barr suggests that Fournier probably used notes taken in Camille Mélinand's class at Lakanal, thus exerting an influence on Eliot in the direction of Bradley and Idealism.

4. Mrs Eliot has confirmed that this refers to a new residence, to which Eliot moved after leaving the rue de l'Université. 'He did live in the rue Saint-Jacques, and in fact took me there on a vist.'

5. This was Fournier's most successful short story, entitled 'Portrait'. Based on a real-life happening, it also harks back to his old obsession with Fromentin's *Dominique.*

REFERENCES

References to the source of quotations are keyed to the following published works:

A *Le Grand Meaulnes*, Livre de Poche, 1983. © A. Fayard.
B *Miracles*, © Éditions Gallimard 1924.
C1, C2 *Correspondance: Jacques Rivière et Alain-Fournier*, 2 vols. 1948. © Éditions Gallimard 1926.
D *Lettres d'Alain-Fournier à sa famille*, Emile-Paul 1949. © Arthème Fayard.
E *Lettres au Petit B*, Emile-Paul 1930. © Arthème Fayard.
F *Correspondance: Alain-Fournier et Charles Péguy*, ed. Yves Rey-Herme, © Arthème Fayard 1973.
G 'Lettres d'Alain-Fournier à Simone', *Le Figaro Littéraire*, 24 September 1964.
H Simone: *Sous de nouveaux soleils*, © Éditions Gallimard 1957.
J Isabelle Rivière: *Vie et Passion d'Alain-Fournier*, Jaspar, Polus et Cie, 1963. © Éditions Alphée.
K Jean Loize: *Alain-Fournier, sa vie et 'Le Grand Meaulnes'*, © Hachette 1968.

9 *I am a peasant*. . . C1, 420
10 *I no longer know*. . . C1, 36
11 *On the road*. . . J, 274
11 *Useless, silent*. . . D, 259
13 *During those first three years*. . . C1, 97
14 *There was never an epoch*. . . C1, 439
14 *I love the Parisian working-man*. . . C1, 359
14 *It must be because I lived*. . . C2, 108
14 *On the day of Mi-Câreme*. . . C2, 69
14 *I saw Isabelle*. . . D, 17, 18
17 *Brest is an old sad town*. . . D, 22
17 *Have I told you*. . . D, 26
17 *For it has rained*. . . K, 37
17 *Suddenly we turned*. . . K, 37
17 *With-her black apron*. . . J, 65
17 *Every morning at 5.30*. . . D, 36
17 *One with a white sunshade*. . . C1, 72
18 *Asnières*. . . C2, 145
32 *For our first year*. . . K, 47
33 *He himself possessed*. . . B, 13-15
35 *M. Racottet*. . . D, 51,52
36 *For the last fortnight*. . . K, 56
36 *You must keep the promise*. . . K, 56
36 *I was so needing you*. . . K, 60, 63
37 *Women are so quick*. . . C1, 207, 208
38ff *Dressed in black*. . . J, 14-18
40 *It was a great shared love*. . . C2, 216
43 *The fields and trees*. . . C1, 11
43 *My little room*. . . C1, 10
43 *The suburban streets*. . . C1, 31,32
43 *When an Englishman*. . . C1, 12

As we prepared for press, new editions either appeared or were announced. They include notably a new version of the *Rivière-Fournier letters* (Gallimard), with notes and an index; a new *Lettres à sa famille* (Fayard), enlarged to include Isabelle's replies; a new *Lettres au Petit B* (Fayard), including eighty or so letters exchanged between René Bichet and his three friends, Fournier, Rivière and Lhote.

INDEX

Bold Type indicates illustrations

PICTURE CREDITS

As already mentioned, most of the artwork comes to us by courtesy of M. Alain Rivière (to whose name may be added that of M. Cahours d'Aspry, director of the Alain-Fournier and Jacques Rivière Museum at the Château de La Chapelle d'Angillon). Acknowledgements also to the Centre Charles Péguy, Orléans (pp. 109, 134), the British Library (128, 136, 139), the National Portrait Gallery (136) and Chiswick Reference Library (47). The painting reproduced on page 109 is by J. P. Laurens. The photographs on pp. 155 and 133 respectively are by Manuel and Dornac. Drawings are by: Félix Vallotton (pp. 41, 75), André Rouveyre (pp. 41, 129, 131), Pierre Payen (pp. 97, 133), and Jean Lebedeff (p. 106). Carcanet Press have made every effort to check copyright owners and apologize for any omissions.